TRUE ENOUGH

A Surgeon's Mostly True Reflections on Life, Medicine, and Marine Navigation

by Alan Muskett MD

DEDICATION

To my blessed mother Bess, who concluded a remarkably successful 88 years in February 2015. She read virtually everything I have ever written, gently correcting grammar and subtly suggesting the lack of propriety in some pieces. A gracious, erudite woman of acute discretion, her savvy understanding of medicine and sense of fun always enriched my career and my writing. Between her and my gentle father, I am left with no excuses, resentment, or childhood trauma—just an overwhelming sense of gratitude.

ACKNOWLEDMENTS

Edited by Phil Jensen PhD
Illustrations by Meghan Spielman
Photography by Paul Ruhter Photography
Design by Accent Print Shop

ABOUT THE AUTHOR

Dr. Alan Muskett is a native of Missoula, Montana, and holds an English degree from Montana State University, which is widely considered to be the nation's leading institution for thoracic and plastic surgeon writers. He graduated from the University of Washington Medical School, and completed a general surgery residency at the University of Utah. He then served a fellowship in cardiothoracic surgery at Washington University in St. Louis, achieving a PTSD degree there. In 1991 he returned to Montana, practicing cardiothoracic and vascular surgery for the next 12 years, accumulating some good book material along the way. In 2003, at the age of 46, he suffered a typical male midlife crisis, and moved to Jackson, Mississippi, to do a plastic surgery residency. In 2005 he returned to Billings, MT and has been in practice in plastic and reconstructive surgery since.

This collection of articles is the second for Dr. Muskett, his first book being the international runaway bestseller *Mostly True*. (A few copies were sold in Canada.) His wife Pamela is his first reader always, and come to think of it, his first wife as well, which is both editorially and financially convenient. His children Sally, Cathy, and Luke are frequent targets for gratuitous humor, but due to the exigencies of educational financing, are tolerant. Dr. Muskett's partners at Billings Plastic Surgery, Drs. Steve Grosso and Jarred McDaniel, are also tolerant, but that has more to do with the necessity for call coverage.

INTRODUCTION]

True Enough is a collection of articles written for the *Billings* (Montana) *Gazette*, in addition to several other pieces either bounced by the *Gazette* or published elsewhere. Several articles are entirely new, particularly the chapter entitled *Characters*.

Mostly True, my first book, went on to become an international runaway bestseller, and was made into a movie starring George Clooney as me.

OK, that is an exaggeration; in fact, an outright lie. There are many more lies in this volume, *True Enough*, but they are not labeled. You must read at your own risk.

Mostly True has been a success, however, because of the thousands of conversations I have had with readers and patients regarding the issues and emotions that affect us all. A chapter in this book deals with my daughter Sally's brain tumor surgery, a subject that I had never dreamed I would be writing about, especially a surgery that didn't go well at all.

I think one of our darkest fears is that we are alone in times of need. My most important goal in writing is to let the reader know that in times of physical, emotional, or spiritual crisis that they are walking a path others have walked, and are thinking what others have thought.

This very profound content is mixed with snarky, irreverent, sarcastic humor. That is so you will put up with my preaching. I fear being boring more than being thought callow.

So look forward to the movie version of *True Enough*. They will have to find another actor, as George is getting a little too old to play me.

CONTENTS

1] MEDICAL LIFE

We all have a voyeuristic tendency—we want to see into the lives of others. The tremendous number of movies, TV shows, novels, and magazine articles on medicine indicate that people are fascinated with the subject and people of medicine. Look at me—I'm cashing in on it, too. Actually, my goals are much nobler: to educate the public, if you believe that.

These articles will provide you with an insider's view of day-to-day medicine, which is likely much more mundane than all that other stuff would indicate. It may not be sexy or shocking, but it is real. Maybe I will write a reality show for insomniacs.

A Lioness in Lycra

Imagine yourself as a water buffalo.

More specifically, a doughy, pale, rather amorphous water buffalo.

Worse yet, you are surrounded by gazelles, elegant and muscular, who move effortlessly across the Serengeti.

Then you see her, a lioness, ready to finish you off...but in Lycra?

No, it is the yoga instructor, very soothingly telling you to place your right heel into your left ear. Her voice sounds far away, and you see, in a detached way, the pallid water buffalo in the mirror, wobbling precariously, snorting for air, thrashing about as if it were trapped in quicksand, torrential sweat obscuring the inevitability of its demise. The lioness murmurs an instruction to stand, spread your legs, and place your face on the floor.

My father was a believer in maintenance. He maintained his soul through prayer and study. He maintained his homes, his tools, and his vehicles. He always checked my oil whenever I came home, and I did everything possible to avoid his censorious looks if I hadn't changed it often enough. He maintained his marriage and his family by assiduous attention and continual efforts at renewal. A Depression child, he felt that if you didn't maintain, you didn't deserve. The Bible said so. Shakespeare said so (Fie, 'tis an unweeded garden!)

After your soul and your family, you most importantly maintained your body. Abuse of your body, in his mind, was sinful, open and shut. Your body is a gift and you take care of it. He swam 40 laps every day for 55 years and lifted weights. He wrote it down. Exercise was sacramental to him, the epitome of stewardship.

I'm in decent shape, but not great. I walk a lot, but that isn't cutting it. I would like better balance, better flexibility, and rather vainly, better definition. I don't like being doughy. I would like to continue to slalom water ski with my killer graphite ski, but I don't want to be removed from the lake in pieces.

I figure I have about 20-25 years of decent physical function left in me, having put on a lot of hard miles already. I am realizing that maintenance is becoming critical. Basically, every bit of ground you give up is unlikely to come back. You need to hang on to it. If you gain weight, you are unlikely to lose it. If you block arteries, they don't unblock. If you don't change the oil, your engine burns up, and you deserved it, and you can darn well walk now, can't you?

I have spoken recently to two women who nursed their husbands through the last, gasping, terminal stages of emphysema. They spent years watching the old boy suffocate, and of course they went nowhere and did nothing. Our health maintenance choices can have devastating effects on other people. It is incredibly selfish to mess yourself up and then expect someone to tend your sorry carcass. I don't worry too much about that, because my wife whips out the living will whenever I get a cold, looking for the euthanasia clause. I intend to disrupt her elaborate widowhood fantasies. I will maintain.

What is kind of cool, when it seems all I see is morbidly obesity sometimes, is to see the magnificently fit and athletic men and women in this yoga class. They are the ones paying health insurance premiums for other people to gobble up. The gazelles also quite discreet, pretending not to notice the water buffalo wobbling and spraying sweat.

I find it ironic that the human soul, with all of its spiritual and intellectuals nuances, its loves and passions, its aspirations and expressions, its towering triumphs and deep despairs, requires a vehicle of meat and bone and blood. Our body, the vessel that contains our soul, is all we have between our mortal existence and the Great Beyond. We must respect and maintain and cherish it or we are merely road kill on the Highway of Life, awaiting the vultures. That's right, put down the doughnut and back slowly away.

The lioness, sculpted in her blue stretch garment, gazes implacably on the water buffalo, knowing how it will end. No hurry.

"Now, stand on your fingertips. And relax."

Graduation

Summer is highly significant in the medical world: medical schools graduate, residencies and internships both begin and end, and wrenching transformation occurs. A young surgical colleague called me last weekend, with two weeks left in his residency, two weeks more of obsequious groveling to the Napoleonic tyrant who is currently his instructor. "Give me something," he said, "to get me through." I advised him to recite the serenity prayer, the one where God grants you the courage to change the things you can, and the wisdom to successfully conceal the body.

In June of 1991 I was finishing my cardiothoracic surgery residency, and at age 34 had basically never been out of school. At 34, most professional athletes are retired, and I was still a "boy" for my own set of whiny, dysfunctional, narcissistic surgical professors. My spirits were not low—they were non-existent, sort of a complete lack of psychological immunity. If I had ever slept I would have dreamed of sleep.

Thus one densely humid St. Louis Saturday night, I was ordered to harvest a heart in some dark little burg in Louisiana. Before I boarded the helicopter that would take me to the airport, the transplant chief, Dr. Pasque, gave me his usual pep talk, his hands clenching my trapezius muscles, his face in mine. His viscous Oklahoma accent was particularly menacing that evening. "Boah, if'n you all don't bring meah a good heart, I jus cut yourn out and use it." His approach to excuses was to deny their existence.

We flew in a nifty red Gulfstream to a very dark and small airport, and ended up in a similarly spooky/noir hospital. The small operating room was crowded with transplant surgeons, mostly all in training (the grunts harvest, the big boys sew them in), and their respective beer coolers to store the organs. The liver team was from Pittsburg (three guys conversing in some Middle Eastern dialect), and the kidney guys were out of Wisconsin. I explained that I would open the chest and get the heart ready to go, and then leave it beating while they got their organs isolated and prepared.

We started the operation, and it quickly seemed to me that the liver guys were talking a great deal, gesturing back and forth. I got the sinking feeling that this was a fairly new experience for them. After a bit, I noticed a fairly large amount of blood welling up in the abdomen. Another bad sign was when the anesthesiologist stood up and peered over the drapes.

4

So now there is more blood, and the pressure, which was a nice 120 systolic, is 100, then 80...60...50. I asked the liver team how they were doing. Oh fine, they said, suctioning fiercely. The pressure lingered around 60, then dumped again. I saw Dr. Pasque running a saw up my chest, using my heart to replace the one I had allowed to die.

I took a clamp, occluded the aorta, and filled the heart with the cold preservative solution. Of course, that meant the blood pressure went to zero and the other doctors were out of business. The room erupted in a storm of protest. I could now recognize some of the words from the liver team. I cut the heart out of the chest, elbowed my way out of an angry blue-gowned mob, and headed for the plane.

Realizing that I had probably ended my career, I longed for a plane crash on the way home.

Of course, Monday morning at 7 A.M., my beeper went off. "The chairman wants to see you immediately." I thought about just walking to my car, driving to Mexico, and getting a job in a venereal disease clinic. I thought that probably 12 years of training would meet their credentialing requirements.

"I've received two very angry phone calls this morning, so far, regarding your behavior on Saturday night. Dr. B in Wisconsin is, of course, livid, although they did save the kidneys. Dr. P in Pittsburg was frankly threatening. They would like you fired."

So this was it. The cruelest joke: survive four years of med school and eight freaking years of surgical indentured servitude, and get axed at the buzzer. Perfect.

I was waiting for the guillotine to fall, but the chairman said nothing, just sort of strangely put a hand to his face, and...was that a tear? His shoulders lurched, and then he dissolved into laughter. "I can't stand either one of those arrogant, bloviating despots. You made a tough call, and you did your job. Consider yourself really severely disciplined."

Dr. Pasque was waiting for me outside, apparently fully aware of the drama. He grabbed my trapezius again like lobster claws. He gave me a savage grin, nothing else, and I realized that I had graduated.

Fridays

If you are a surgeon, Fridays are nominally the end of the scheduled workweek, but carry the vaguely menacing threat of heretofore-unplanned mayhem.

Someone enjoying an early and alcoholic start to their weekend, unfettered by the mundanity of seatbelt, exits their F150 at 80 miles per hour and engages in a passionate clutch with a fencepost.

Patients, anxious about the approaching weekend and the perceived unavailability of their provider, call offices in droves.

Poorly understood, dark, karmic forces, particularly manifest on Fridays, induce heart attacks and GI bleeds and hip fractures in inordinate numbers.

Observe a surgeon on a Friday, and you see a faint wince each time their beeper or cell phone chirps.

My Friday started with a minor procedure in the office under local anesthesia. No antibiotics, no sedation, just local. Before we even started (maybe it was the prep solution that caused an allergic reaction?!), the patient developed severe laryngospasm, which means the voice box and the airway clamped shut. The patient couldn't breathe, the oxygen level plummeted, and the heart rate became irregular.

Fortunately, I had two very experienced nurses (note I didn't say "old war horses," a term previously used to ill effect) with me who quickly located everything I needed to break the spasm and restore the airway. But I am sure another chunk of my personal myocardium necrosed in the process.

My big reconstruction case at the hospital was delayed because the OR room to which I was assigned was occupied by a patient who had had surgery the day before and who had developed intraabdominal bleeding as a result of it being Friday.

In the room next to me, the surgeons were performing a biopsy on a lung tumor, which inconveniently was adherent to the main pulmonary artery, which contains most of the blood in the world. When the tumor came out, part of the pulmonary artery came with it, and the resultant deluge of dark blood led to some very unpleasant but fortunately retrievable commotion.

Down the hall, the aforementioned driver/pilot was having his spleen removed and his cracked liver assuaged while a band of anesthesiologists and nurses poured the offerings of about 30 big-hearted blood donors into his pickled circulation.

Most jobs, on a day-to-day basis, aren't that hard. I've said that I could train a chimpanzee with decent parents to do most of what I do. When the economy is hot, anyone can sell cars or boats or houses. If the weather is great and the other team is lousy, sure, you will win all your games.

What separates the men from the boys, the women from the girls, and the professionals from the poseurs, are the tough times. It is the Fridays when things are unscripted and out of control and wholly unpredictable. When the economy is lousy, when the patient is angry, when the blood is gushing, and when your head is clamped in a vice and your gut is a boa constrictor trying to crush your soul—that is when you find out who the pros are.

Blessedly it doesn't happen very often. But that's what you prepare for all those years—those years of study and harsh experience, of boredom and terror, of dreams and doubt. Because you never really know when Friday might come.

I think I will take Friday off.

Dock Surgery

I recently worked with orthopedic surgeon Jim Elliot on a patient with a really smashed up ankle. She had broken all kinds of bones, and then the skin around the ankle had died off. Jim would fix up the bones, and then I would figure out a way to cover it all up with muscle or skin or spackling compound.

He gave me a nice tour of the ankle joint while asking me to pull and yank and grunt the pieces into place, and then hold them while he popped in the screws and plates. It was interesting to see how this fits into that, and to see the maze of ligaments that holds it all together. I think we got a very usable ankle out of the effort, although I won't be putting a picture of it in my cosmetic propaganda.

Weeks later, on a brilliant August evening in the Swan Valley, I was making dinner while overlooking the glimmering lake, now composing itself after being shredded by skiers and surfers all day.

In addition to a beef burgundy sauce with mushrooms and shallots, I was also composing a pitcher of "lemonade," the kind best kept away from an open flame. I mix this up in an elegant carafe called the "Bubba Keg."

A harried young woman appeared at the door. "Come down to the dock—Dad's been hurt!"

"Dad" is Roger, my lifelong lake buddy, a ripped physical specimen and a maniac water skier. He had caught the tip of his graphite-wonder, double-booted slalom ski, and had violently wrenched both legs.

Roger wasn't looking too good, being carried by a couple of stout young men onto the dock. He'd been in the water for a while, and with the pain of the injury was looking a little shocky.

It was also apparent that his right ankle was way, way wrong. The bone stuck way out on the side, and a tendon was bow-strung across it.

A dislocation of this nature can lead to significant disability later on if it is not reduced quickly. (I sort of knew that, but after I Googled and YouTubed it later, it turned out to be true.) I told Roger I thought I could reduce it, but that it would be nothing short of barbaric. "Do it," was his calm response.

I ran up to the cabin to get some sort of wrap and some ice. My friend Chuck had brought us a first aid kit 15 years ago, and sure enough, there was an ace wrap and the most perfect malleable splint you ever saw. I felt bad that I had no kind of useful sedative or pain medication. I then eyed the "Bubba Keg."

Calculating the dose at about half a tumbler, I returned to my patient, who remained remarkably stoical. I employed Bill, Roger's brother, to assist me.

Bill and Roger own an IT-services company that employs 160 people. They are conservative, disciplined men with lovely families. They were, of course, teenage orangutan party animals, and had a bad influence on me, an otherwise irreproachable youth. We have enough history to assure mutual discretion.

I had Bill pull longitudinally on the leg while I maneuvered the ankle bone up and over into the socket. Again, I pushed and grunted, only this time in 90-degree heat. After rather unmercifully hard mashing, and for a protracted period, the bone just glided into place. The splint was applied to hold the reduction, the "Bubba Keg" redosed, and the patient carried up the hill for a ride to the ER.

I am intrigued by life's funny little grace notes. Right before I went to the lake, I got a tour of the ankle joint, really understanding the anatomy for the first time. Then, a 15-year-old first aid kit has the perfect splint. And, of course, standing by quietly and loyally was "Bubba Keg."

When you are no longer open to new information, new ideas, or new skills, you are old. And very possibly annoying, as well. To say "I'm hopeless with computers" or "I can't cook" and "I can't hammer a nail" is often a way of saying "I'm intellectually lazy." Very few things in life are that hard to learn. Usually it is just a matter of pushing and grunting.

That being said, if you dislocate your ankle, and you are not 80 miles away in a forest, go see a real doctor.

Hospital Food

Since the age of 16 or so I would guess I have had 25% of my meals in a health care facility. Beginning as an orderly at St. Pat's in Missoula, and over the years in Bozeman, Seattle, Salt Lake, St. Louis, Jackson (Mississippi), and various parts of Central America, I've eaten in hospital cafeterias, snack bars, and call rooms. If an expert food critic were needed to evaluate hospital cuisine, I would qualify.

Criticizing hospital food is an easy, clichéd exercise. I like hospital food.

The two critical elements of fine dining are 1) I don't have to make it, and 2) I don't have to do the dishes. Everything beyond that is ill-defined brown-gray gravy.

I eat at work only if I am really hungry and in a hurry. The fact that the chicken breast is a little desiccated from a long stretch on the steam table just makes you chew more thoroughly. I had lunch recently with a young surgeon, recently out of training, and he devoured two entrees, a salad, and two sides in ninety seconds while carrying on a conversation. Oh, and while texting the whole time, as well.

You have to learn to work the cafeteria. The server lady when I was an orderly long ago would give me this withering, baleful, condescending stare when I came down the line, never asking what I wanted, just staring, and I would croak out my request. The size of a small house with a naval tattoo on her forearm, she would then contemptuously splat down a tablespoon of "mushroom soup tuna noodle casserole" on my plate, and dare me to say something. Too timid, I never did.

My younger brother, on the other hand, would say "Margaret, could I have you for lunch?" and give her the most lascivious, frankly suggestive look a high school boy could deliver, and she would just shovel it on.

In residency, my friend Jake would always order two chicken breasts with lots of gravy, and then use the gravy to obscure the second breast so he would only get charged for one.

Remember that on those food bars, they often weigh things. Chicken wings, the non-gooey ones, don't weigh much. Salads can kill you.

If you wonder why hospitals crank out the burgers and curly fries and deep-fried cheese nuggets, it isn't because they haven't tried nutritionally correct offerings. They have made great efforts to prepare healthy foods, and virtually no one buys it.

I am amused when patients complain about food. As an orderly, I used to carry trays of the tuna noodle casserole off a big cart, and now they have "room service," and you order off a menu. My feeling is that your job as a patient is to get out of the hospital as quickly as possible, and then you can resume the gourmet meals you are presumably cooking for yourself at home. Let's be honest—a cheeseburger on a beach in Hawaii is going to taste better than a cheeseburger after your prostatectomy.

To me, there is no bad food short of salmonella poisoning. There are probably at least a billion people on this planet whose lives are dominated by chronic hunger. I am so grateful that I am not hungry, and that nor are my children. On the cleft lip missions I've done in Central America, the families of the patients are provided a very basic meal during their stay, and watching them tear into the beans and rice is sobering.

In my cardiac residency, we had a group function at a very fancy St. Louis restaurant, and they served "squab," which was this tiny little bird, like a baby pigeon, which apparently is a super-cool dish. Artfully arranged were two miniscule bits of some exotic potato, and then a vegetable, equally scarce, I had never heard of. I think with the room and everything they charged the department 100 bucks a plate. We had to stop at White Castle on the way home.

Now compare this with the hospital chili-cheese-dog bar. They have these one-pound franks, all the chili and cheese you can pile on, and best of all, *they don't weigh it*. If they only served Miller Lite on draft, why, you'd be there.

I live in an area blessed with many great restaurants run by talented professionals, and I enjoy them. But I would have to say, my heart is still on the steam table, and probably always will be.

Changes

I was 22 months old when my parents brought home a pink little prune-looking bundle that they announced as my new baby brother.

I quickly noted that this alarming new presence was seemingly glued to my mother, and hogged the attention that previously had been mine.

After two weeks, I told my parents, "Take him back!"

Change is tough.

This weekend, our office had yet another retirement party, this time for our beloved Cindy, who is dumping us after 35 years to pursue her own selfish goals of travel and adventure with her husband, rather than managing our business, solving our problems, and placating my tantrums.

And then there was dear Diane, with whom I did hundreds of hearts and with whom I would later work for a decade in plastic surgery. I told her, "Big deal, you are 60-something and have worked forever." There is nobility in dropping in the fields with the plow around your neck.

Kayrene, another 30-plus-year veteran, left us for quilts and her garden. Now, my go-to, third-down-receiver nurse, Trish, wants to go part-time for the feeble excuse that she has two teenagers and a baby—one who can magically conjure a fever at daycare and make mommy come running.

Parenthetically, fevers in babies are no big deal. Mothers get all worked up over fevers, but I found that by setting the little troublemaker outside in a high chair (most fevers are in the winter, after all) until their lips are very slightly blue, the fever is magically gone. Sometimes a football game would distract me, and the little tyke might be a tad stiff, but a couple of minutes fluffing in the dryer and it's back to normal. Parenting, and medicine for that matter, just aren't that hard.

If babies weren't so good for my business, what with tummy tucks and breast lifts and all, I'd secretly mix Depo-Provera (birth control) in all my Botox injections.

We begin a job as a way to make a living, and then find that those workplace relationships form an essential part of our lives. Working with team members to save a life or to restore a broken person to wellness creates an intimacy matched nowhere else than perhaps the battlefield. As these remarkable women move on, both the pride and the ache are exquisite.

I've replenished the faithless retirees by shamelessly stealing the best and brightest from other practices and hospitals. This is not a nice thing to do, and I feel sorta bad about it sometimes. I get over it quickly.

Ten years ago my partner Steve Grosso and I were in a little bitty office with five employees, and now we have built a building, have already remodeled that, and have had to buy more land to expand the parking lot. So now we are up (I'm guessing here) to 14 employees, a seven-figure mortgage, and a third surgeon, Dr. Jerrod McDaniel, a very affable and capable young man whose father is about my age. Yikes.

Most people, myself included, think that change is about equal parts excitement and anxiety. I had this vision long ago that someday I would be done "getting there" and just cruise. But most careers, and especially medicine, won't allow that. I constantly have to learn new techniques, new drugs, new federal regulations, and new ways to manage my business and practice. Now I'm forced to relive a childhood trauma, because just like my baby brother, everyone in the office will give the new surgeon all the attention.

Oh, to live forever in the cocoon of comfort, the sunshine of security, and the blessing of the familiar. To sit at the kitchen table in our house on Hollis Street in Missoula and eat Mom's oatmeal cookies and drink milk and talk about my day at school.

But I must be aware, as must we all, that the richness of lives, the wealth of our experience, comes from the changes that force us to grow.

The joy that I realize from an elegantly performed operation arises from the forge of failure. New and enriching relationships have occurred due to the loss of others. New buildings and tools and partners and even parking lots are rewarding and risky and exciting and terrifying.

Hamlet wondered, "To be, or not be, that is the question."

If we want to "be"—to be players, to engage in our lives—we are going to take some hits, take some risks, and see change as a constant driver of growth rather than a threat.

I am blessed to have my mother yet with me at 87, and I asked her, in retrospect, if it wouldn't, after all, have been a good idea to take my brother "back." She allowed that since he was a successful physician, husband, father, and devoted son that no, she wouldn't take him back.

She suggested another remedy.

"Get over it."

Stylin'

Way back in my nurse's-aide days I took care of a guy named Jerry. He had been basically cut in half by a train, both his legs amputated at the hip, and somehow had managed to survive. He was constantly septic from breakdown of his hip wounds, pressure sores on his back, and his necessary urostomy bags. He more or less lived in the hospital.

His attending physician was Dr. W, kind of a riverboat gambler dandy, who had a huge practice based on unshakeable confidence and a sort of greasy charm. He rarely saw Jerry, and in fairness there was little he could do to mitigate Jerry's predicament. Jerry worshiped Dr. W, and I mentioned shyly one day to Dr. W that his patient would appreciate a visit.

Dr. W huffed, but realized it had been a while, so he stepped into Jerry's room, thrust out his arm with an extended middle finger, and robustly added the lyrics. He left without another word. Jerry cackled in delight.

Later that summer I took care of a guy in the ER. We stabilized him and called the cardiologist. After a while the ER doctor asked me if Dr. S had arrived, so I checked the room. I went back to the desk and reported that no, the doctor wasn't there, but there was some homeless dude who looked like a billy goat in there with the patient. "Good," they replied, "that's Dr. S."

Fascinated, I returned to the room to check it out. Dr. S had the patient's hand between both of his. "Hey Earl," he said in a voice of merino fleece, "you ain't bull... me now, are you?" Earl's wrenching anxiety, the taste of death in his mouth, and the trembling dread in his limbs dissipated. "You're here, Doc. I'll be fine."

Dr. S looked right at you, listening intently as if he had all the time in the world. You felt better just talking about the weather. He was also a technical genius in the cath lab, and undoubtedly the richest billy goat in Montana.

14

In 40 years of observing physicians, nurses, and all other health care professionals, I have seen every style imaginable. I was getting totally abused in the ER one night during training—a guy who had been shot in the hand spitting and kicking at me, to say nothing of the verbal abuse. My fellow resident and buddy Jake, a Russian immigrant from Brooklyn, wandered in and shook his head. "Big gansta, are we? Let me show you how the Russian mob does it back home." He proceeded to "examine" the hand in a way that greatly improved cooperation.

I worked with one surgeon who was so awful with patients and families that he hired a lovely woman to do the talking. He had the hands of God, so it worked for everybody. Another guy would come into the exam room, describe his dental appointment in detail, and then leave without asking the patient a single question.

Some docs are formal and dignified, and many patients like that because they feel a grown-up is treating them. Some docs are that way because they are still the smartest kid in high school with no social skills.

As a patient, find a style that fits yours.

My style is a compilation of little bits of the thousands of providers with whom I have worked. I tend to be a little irreverent, because I think most everyone is anxious when they go to a doctor. Patients are also very astute when it comes to distinguishing between a slick, pre-programmed act and genuine caring. I want a person to leave our office less anxious, better educated, and loved up a little.

My style doesn't suit everyone. Some think it is a bit flip to tell a 71-year-old woman facing bilateral mastectomy and reconstruction that she will have the hottest set in Miles City, Montana. Sometimes a patient will ask to see my partner Steve or go somewhere else. Despite my bruised feelings, I don't feel that they are humorless dweebs.

My all-time favorite stylist was a nurse named Celestine who worked with me in a public clinic in Jackson, Mississippi, during my plastics training. I was seeing another gunshot wound in follow-up, a too-cool guy who had been been shot in the face, and had been quite magnificently reconstructed, if I don't say so myself. He wouldn't take out his headphones, would mumble responses, and basically couldn't be bothered.

Celestine walked in on this scene and erupted. She smote those headphones with a fury that left him fortunate to have ears at all.

"You all sit up straight and get that ridiculous hat off in here. You look the man in the eye and answer him with respect or the other side of your sorry #$% face is getting caved in."

"Yes ma'am." Now that's stylin'.

ReviewMe.com

As soon as I walk into the room I can tell she isn't right. Normally upbeat and effusive, she sits tensely on the exam table. Has she developed an infection or a wound separation? Is she disappointed in the result of her breast reconstruction, which, in my modest opinion, is somewhere between righteous and awesome?

So what's up?

A torrent of tears and words and mucous reveals the answer. The lymph nodes we removed during the course of mastectomy and reconstruction have unexpectedly shown more cancer. There will be additional radiation and chemotherapy. Her prognosis is less clear. Her children are yet small.

This 10-minute, routine follow-up visit turns into 40 minutes of listening and support.

My next patient is a new consultation who was scheduled at 8:15 and is still cooling her heels at 9:00. She had hoped to be back at work by then, but now it will be 10:00. I don't blame her for being miffed.

So imagine both these patients go to their computers later that day to write a review for a medical website. The first patient might say I was compassionate and interested, and the second would say I was rude. Five stars here, one star there.

I am not a technophobe by any means. Our practice has a blazing-fast, state-of-the-art electronic record that only slows us down to about half-speed. We try every laser, ultrasound, radiofrequency, heat-em-up and freeze-em-down, fat-busting, wrinkle-erasing, and cellulite-eliminating machine that comes along. Most don't work beyond the initial three-month placebo blush. On the other hand, email and texted photographs have been wonderful for taking care of patients in Ekalaka.

I am struggling a bit with the whole online evaluation process. Whether it is surgery or hotels or boat charters, there is a whole industry of Internet-based reviews.

I would like to ignore it. I would like my patients and my referring physicians to talk to other patients and physicians personally and render their opinion.

I think reviews vary tremendously depending on whether the reviewer is identified. Someone identified as WHZBNGR66 can say anything they want online, but Alan Muskett has to think about it a little. I noticed our local paper went to using a Facebook account for online comments, which changed the dialogue completely.

Who is more likely to write a review? I would expect a mad person rather than a happy one. Is that, then, a meaningful resource? One guy chartered an expensive boat and the toilet plugged. He must have written ten scathing reviews of the company, which have been hanging around for years.

You can hire services to manage your online reviews, and if you get a sour apple you can overwhelm it with positive reviews. I would just prefer to identify the sour apple and burn their house down. That probably costs more.

I do appreciate the patients who take the time to give me feedback. There are times, despite our systems and protocols, that we miss phone calls, give inadequate instructions, or just miss a patient's concern. I appreciate the chance to apologize or to fix a deficiency in our process. Having my tail chewed in person is humbling, and it makes me work harder to avoid it in the future. That means so much more than a random potshot on the interweb.

Of course, in some conflicts with patients, I think I am right and they are wrong. One guy had had several failed procedures for a wound, and I was asked to see him. He was a heavy tobacco user, and I told him we could do nothing for him until he cut out the tobacco. He said it had nothing to do with the wound. I said, "OK, you're not diabetic, you have good circulation—no immunosuppressant, what do you think?" He thought I was flip and condescending, and I'm sure he could write a whopper of a review. I think he does not want to give up tobacco. Find another surgeon. That happens. I'm not right all the time, but neither is the patient.

How about this? HusbandReview.com. If you asked my wife to write a review about me, should it be after I finally gave her an engagement ring after 30 years (five stars), or after I inadvertently referred to her bathing suit cover-up as a "muu muu?" (Are there negative stars?) DadReview.com. Right after I nixed the spring break trip to Vegas? Maybe not.

So what to do? Rather than chasing electronic phantoms around the ether, I will recommit to the person in front of me. Not the screen, not the iPhone, not the text or tweet. I will use my actual ears and hands and heart to give the one person in front of me all I have in attention, intellect, and heart.

Somewhere online is a place for comments. Please write that I am awesome. Don't forget to use lots of stars.

Toward Big-Time Medicine

I had several stuffed bears as a child. One was Cinnamon Bear, who had a cool music box in his chest, which made a light tinkling noise when the bear was moved. When the music box quit working, I cut the bear's chest open and removed the box, which a kind jeweler then repaired. The box was replaced, and the wound sutured as neatly as one would expect from a six-year-old.

This procedure had two results. I earned a visit to a pediatrician, a different one, one who had no white coat or stethoscope, and seemed to just want to talk. He told my mother not to worry: I would either be a serial killer or a surgeon, but it was too early to tell. He suggested she keep an eye on the neighborhood pets.

The other result was a career-making revelation. I learned that people actually had jobs where you could cut open not only bears, but people, and fix them. When I met Missoula's first heart surgeon, who had a hot blonde girlfriend and a red Turbo Carrera, well, there you go.

My entire focus beginning in grade school and throughout my school days was on becoming a surgeon. My eighth-grade science fair project was on anti-arrhythmic drugs. Even the judges thought that insufferable.

I've not regretted my decision. I wonder at times that if I had taken a similar dedication and intensity to Wall Street, I would have a 120-foot yacht in Ft. Lauderdale, and a couple of brief stints in a minimum security facility (as opposed to four years of medical school and 10 years of residency).

One thing I think the Wall Street guys struggle with is meaning. What am I doing with my life? Does my life matter?

I suffer anxiety from bad outcomes, worry over the ever-present legal threats, and struggle at times to keep my mouth shut. But I don't wonder if what I do is meaningful. The most significant thing you can ever do in life is relieve the suffering of another person.

So the explosion of health care education in Billings and the surrounding region pleases me. Rocky Mountain College now graduates 30 students a year in the Physician Assistant program. Montana State nursing students and University of Washington medical students are ubiquitous in local hospitals. We have naturopathic students and residents. Physical therapy, occupational therapy, speech therapy—if it's therapeutic, we have someone studying it. Local schools train surgical techs and CNAs.

Rural areas (I guess that's us) often struggle for primary care providers. Everyone wants to be an anesthesiologist in Seattle. So the development of the Family Practice Residency, and more recently the Internal Medicine Residency, in this area is highly significant. Most doctors tend to hang around the area where they trained, and many of our local primary care stars were trained here.

You will probably notice, whether as a hospital patient or in the clinic, that you will be seeing more students. Be patient. If you have to tell the same story 36 times or get a little extra prodding, be cool. You are now in one of the big-time medical centers, which are all training facilities.

The burgeoning medical education landscape here presents wonderful opportunities for children and grandchildren. If you want to have the attention you deserve when you are dribbling applesauce down your bib in the nursing home, your offspring need good jobs to bring them home. All three of my children have chosen health careers, and although I don't see them contributing to my yacht fund, I am proud of their choices.

If you look at surveys evaluating communities or cities, medical care is always near the top of the list of concerns. Our area is moving to the big time with broader and more sophisticated care, (maybe more aggravation at times), and expanded opportunities for our youth.

So if your little one starts carving up their stuffed animals, well, keep an eye on them. Who knows what could happen.

The Cartel

You wouldn't think that the specialty of plastic surgery is infiltrated by organized crime, but it is.

I was recently shaken down by the "AMBPLS cartel," also known as the American Board of Plastic Surgery. It has been almost 10 years since I received by board certification in plastic surgery, so it was time to renew my certificate.

The gangsters started by requesting my $200 annual fee, which is apparently used to take out my certificate and dust it. Then, as part of the "pre-certification screening," I had to submit records on my surgical cases, which they would review for 225 bucks.

Congratulations came in an email—I could now apply to take the test. 450 dollars to review the application, and of course I had to submit every license, facility privilege, letter of recommendation, fifth-grade English score, and dental flossing diary for the last 10 years.

Further success! I can take the test! Oh, and send us 1,250 smackers, as well.

So I settled down to study. Since I had taken the $650 "in-training assessment exam" the year before, I felt pretty good about my preparation. I pulled out that highly valuable syllabus and began studying.

Not long after came another email. An "all-new" board review course was offered, and the message strongly implied that the questions they sold you last year for $650 were about as good as an implant with a hole in it. They STRONGLY RECOMMENDED that I purchase this $495 course—wink, wink—and do so promptly.

I stared at that email for quite a long time. It was like facing down some hood outside your store, who was telling you how much of a shame it would be if those nice windows were to get broken.

I paid up. I studied those 500 questions over and over.

Finally the big day came. I went to the test place, did the strip search, and took my 200-question, four-hour exam.

Which I finished in 50 minutes. I still can't figure out how I got four wrong. The questions were VERY familiar. Sometimes the easiest route is just to pay the protection money.

Health care is a gigantic business in this country. Where fortunes can be made, opportunists flock like teenage boys to an Xbox.

Pharmaceutical companies, insurance companies, health care conglomerates, these testing rackets, continuing education, the whole legal/liability industry—everyone and their dog is selling shovels and pans to the miners.

(Note: Provider incomes are flat to lower. I have to endure the shame of renting a boat when I go the San Juan Islands.)

We aren't victims here. As patients, we want the best: the newest, the latest, the most expensive, and we want it NOW.

None of this generic, waiting list, reasonable algorithm-driven Canadian unleaded health care for me. Make it a double.

My strategy is this: Do not get sick. You can't afford it. Many, but of course not all, health care expenditures can be avoided.

Doctors see way more fluffy people than they do stringy jack rabbit-types. If you go from a size 16 to a size 8, you will have to buy new clothes, but you won't have to buy an $80,000 coronary bypass or a $35,000 hip.

Blood pressure and cholesterol, seat belts, cigarettes, healthy diet— we all know the impact of those on our health. Another sermon. Yawn.

So forget the health consequences and consider your financial ruin. Insurance costs have jumped 20% after the initiation of Obamacare, and your employer is going to take that chunk out of your oversized behind. There won't be any money left for your wages.

We all need to shape up and quit wasting money on health care, when we could be wasting it on yachts, table saws, and a tractor with awesome hydraulics.

Every vulture on the planet, including the American Board of Plastic Surgery, has its beak in the health care carcass. Your job is to keep your carcass off the highway so the poor vultures don't get so fat they can't fly.

How do I know all this? I've been studying non-stop for the last year. I would be happy to sell you all the answers.

2) I'M WATCHING YOUR BACK

I grew up thinking, but more hoping, that medicine was something of a priesthood. When I first started hanging around doctors and hospitals, there was a sanctimonious atmosphere. As a nurse's aide, I stood up when the doctor entered the nurse's station. The doctors got free food in the cafeteria and free drugs from the pharmacy. There was a strict prohibition on advertising, as it was considered coarse and vulgar. Doctors smoked in the lounge. I thought it was all pretty cool.

Medicine has discovered the magic of marketing, of flim-flam, and the power of perception over reality. "Five-Star" heart programs and "Top-100" orthopedic programs can be terrible.

One of my goals in these articles is to provide an "insider's" view of the workings of medicine—not necessarily cynical, but let's say pragmatic. I want you to understand that a lot of medical information is erroneous hype. I also want you to understand that there are a whole lot of providers who care a great deal about you.

Conspiracy

A new study published in the *Journal of the American Medical Association (JAMA)* reported that half of Americans believe in at least one medical conspiracy.

An example: The government knows cell phones cause brain cancer but are pressured by the companies to cover up the evidence. Agree 20%, not sure 40%, disagree 40%. Other theories: the government suppressing cancer cures to aid drug companies, the CIA using the AIDS virus, vaccines causing autism, and so forth.

As one who believes in and participates in several medical conspiracies, this study made me very nervous. The stark light of truth is exposing those of us on the inside.

The problem with this study is that they missed all the good conspiracies.

The ones about cell phones and autism coming from vaccines are so lame. Here's how I know: Every pediatrician on the planet has their kid vaccinated. No matter how cold and conspiratorial you are, you don't screw up your own kid. As for cell phones, neither of my daughters has brain cancer. Besides, everyone texts now. Case closed.

So what are the really juicy conspiracies?

Doctors tell everyone to quit smoking. They don't do that so you will be healthy. The British National Health Service found that smokers actually consume far fewer resources in their lifetime. That's because they're dead sooner. You see, we doctors make way more money off you if you hang around and get old and senile. I can't do facelifts on smokers, either, especially dead ones.

Drug companies do try to influence your drug use in a big way. They spend fortunes advertising for testosterone patches, erectile-dysfunction drugs, and meds for everything from arthritis to baldness. It works, too. A patient comes to me and says, "Hey, Doc, how about that new drug Zeboofa, the one for curing your slice with the seven iron?" I say, "Sure, I'll write you a scrip for that. It's 21 dollars a pill." No thanks, Doc.

I hardly ever write a prescription for a new drug, because they are all hideously expensive. Two Motrin and two beers will fix most things, anyway. That's just between you and me, though. I don't want to lose my drug-company bribes.

We doctors have a meeting once a year to decide on all the newest conspiracies and secret plans. That's when we put secret transmitters in artificial hips and encode commercial messages in pacemakers. One brilliant and really cheap idea was to make consent forms so impossibly long that no one would ever read them.

So what should we believe? Recent, very well done studies have shown that eating organic, pesticide- and hormone-free food has no influence on health outcomes. Similarly, vitamins and supplements have no effect on health. Aspirin prevents heart attacks only in known heart patients. Last week, it was the research that saturated fats are now probably OK. Pass the bacon.

Next will be the revelation that Santa Claus is a wife-beating crack head.

Most of my medical practice is based on evidence-based science, but I never discount a patient's belief system. I have my own. I believe in the magic of huckleberries, and I am sure that Excedrin is better than the generic form.

I have great respect for my patients of faith. Studies show they survive and tolerate illnesses better than those without a faith structure. But don't substitute prayer for vaccination or treatment of your kid's diabetes. Even God thinks you're an idiot. I know. We email.

In a similar manner, if being vegan or eating a shovelful of supplements a day makes you feel well, then you are well. Wellness is way beyond molecules and cells and pills. All the scientific studies I mentioned above haven't made a dent in the sales of organic foods or supplements. But don't expect a food or a pill to substitute for hauling your wide rear away from the table and out onto the road.

As we broaden our concept of health to include an overall wellness, we must necessarily address the mystery that is faith, whether it is in our religion, our food, our pill-shaped talismans, or our conspiratorial theories.

And that's okay. Mystery is what makes our lives dimensional and colorful. Mystery is beauty without explanation. Why does eating huckleberries directly from the bush deep in a sun-dappled, high-mountain forest help me get through the months of darkness? Why, when I first saw that damp little baby, was my heart gone forever?

I don't need to know.

But Wait—There's More....

This last month the LifeStyle Facelift company ceased operations and will likely declare bankruptcy. Lifestyle spent $70 million a year advertising a "revolutionary one-hour facelift" under local anesthesia with, of course, amazing results at a low price. Their spokeswoman, one-hit wonder Debbie Boone, said the operation would "light up your life."

I actually attended a LifeStyle recruitment session for surgeons at one of our national plastic surgery meetings. Many people had responded to the glowing infomercials and had returned from a "LifeStyle Center" with problems that needed fixing. I thought I would check it out.

Their system was this: The prospective patient calls the 800 number and makes an appointment. They meet not with a doctor or a nurse, but with a salesman who is trained to look for various sagging parts. The salesman then "upsells" the patient—that is, adds on eyelids, brow lift, etc. Kind of like that "protection package" that about doubles the cost of the car you thought you got a good deal on.

After meeting the salesman and paying for the procedure, a surgical date is set. The surgeon meets the patient for the first time in preop, then does as much as he/she can in the time allowed, 90 minutes, unless there were "upgrades."

The recruitment session for surgeons sort of looked like an AA meeting. The prospective LifeStyle magicians were pretty down on their luck: practices failing, recession victims, competition in urban areas wearing them down. The recruiter extolled LifeStyle as a great place for surgeons, because you didn't have to talk to patients, just operate with no overhead.

Of course, the surgeon got only 15% of the total fee. The salesman got more than the surgeon. We were told that you made up for the low reimbursement by operating fast and doing a lot of cases. They expected you to do four facelifts a day for four days a week.

The surgeons were told to do whatever they knew how to do for 90 minutes, and the surgeons certainly hadn't seen the ads on TV where there were no incisions and amazing results. No wonder, then, when states' attorneys general across the country were kept quite busy by angry consumers.

I am quite an efficient operator. I don't like the term "fast surgeon," as it implies speed as a goal, but I did most of my hearts in less than two and a half hours, and I also move along as a plastics guy. Facelifts demand precision and concentration and care, and I can't do even the most basic lift in 90 minutes. Doing four a day for four days a week would leave me babbling in a psych ward.

I think consumers rarely get taken any more by car deals, home sales, or a refrigerator purchase. There is too much information out there on products and prices and quality. But medicine isn't there yet. I can tell you that all these "Five-Star" ratings, "Ranked #1 for Hemorrhoid Care," and "Best in the State for Not Killing You" billboards and ads and smiling photographs are all bogus. For only 189 dollars (standard, not premium-level), I can be "America's Top Plastic Surgeon."

LifeStyle isn't the only national health care vendor. I see "Cancer Centers of America" ads all the time. I don't know anything about them, good or bad, but I do know we have two comprehensive cancer centers in Billings, MT, who are doing all the same latest and greatest things. The computerized algorithms we get from the national cancer institutes are updated daily, so everyone is essentially dealing from the same deck. If some institution has a super cool new treatment we don't have, we send them there, but that is unusual.

Rather than seeking medical care on the Shopping Channel, establish a relationship with a good primary care provider. Find someone who will talk to you, someone with whom you have rapport. Then, if something comes up, ask them to tell you whom you should see for a hip replacement or a breast reduction.

Most of my patients come from other patients. "I want exactly what she had" is a frequent comment. If a number of your acquaintances are happy with a particular surgeon, that surgeon is probably OK. Weigh carefully the isolated negative review, as everyone has bad outcomes at times. Look at the general consensus.

Now that LifeStyle has folded, I am going to fill the void with Muskett'sMagicMakeover. For only $19,999.99, I will fix not only your face, but also every sag you have (anesthesia, sutures, bandages, and surgeon vodka not included). If you call in the next 30 minutes, you get a free Botox (expired) treatment.

But wait—there's more....

Megatron

Big surgical meetings are a study in contrast: meeting rooms filled with staid scientific droning and the carnival-like ruckus of the exhibit hall. You've been to conventions—they all seem to have the exhibit hall—where busty babes and gel-haired dudes let you know, in a conspiratorial just-you-and-me tone, that your business, indeed your entire existence in the marketplace, is over—done—unless you purchase their app, machine, instrument, device, service, etc. Which, by the way, your competitor is looking at closely. To pass on their product leaves visions of your gaunt, hungry children in rags, your office shuttered, shrouded in weeds, and your wife riding away in said competitor's Beemer, purchased with the bounty realized by his astute judgment in the exhibit hall.

One "senior" laser salesman, whom I think I recognized from my daughter's recent college graduation, was extolling the virtues of the Megatron Eliminator XLE. He exhorted me to attend the session of the meeting moderated by Dr. Lazar Beame, "the foremost figure in the field." Apparently the Megatron laser restores youth, beauty, virility, and math skills with a brief treatment that involves no recovery, or "down time."

Each speaker at a scientific session is required to disclose any industry connection, royalties, stipends, etc. The speakers usually have a slide right at the beginning of the talk that lists their disclosures. That slide appears for exactly 0.000001 seconds, so there is no chance you can actually read what goodies the makers of the Megatron are sending Dr. Beame's way.

Dr. Beame shows amazing results with the Megatron: haggard patients with big jowls and turkey necks transformed into smooth, smart looking wonders. He became very irritated when one of the audience members pointed out that perhaps the facelift the patient had at the same time of the Megatron treatment might have had something to do with the result. He became nearly apoplectic when another guy asked him what happened to the Light Saber laser, which Dr. Beame was extolling just last year.

There has been a great deal of concern on the part of the government and many health care institutions about the undue influence of the medical industry on the behavior of medical providers. Many organizations, including some in my area, won't let medical salespeople meet with providers.

Medical companies are now going direct to consumers, as you well know. "Ask your doctor about Wondra, a new drug to treat depression, obesity, laziness, and general crabbiness." The surgical-equipment companies suggest to the patient that unless their prostate is removed by a robot, their urologist is probably a knuckle-dragging Neanderthal.

So what do I believe? What should you believe?

I make decisions regarding devices and drugs very simply. Is there real scientific evidence, not just a nice brochure? Does it work when I use it? Can my patients afford it? Those three questions kill about 90% of the ideas I evaluate.

The idea that a post-adolescent, skinny-jean dude will unduly influence me is unlikely. I would strongly suspect that your filter for sales pitches of all kinds is fairly sharp, as well.

I am a pitchman. My patients often come in with little medical knowledge, listen to a fairly complex presentation—say, regarding breast reconstruction—and make remarkably astute judgments.

We hear clichés all the time about how "the media forces us to starve ourselves to meet the ideal of the skinny model." One lap around Wal-Mart perusing elastic-banded sweat pants pretty much disproves that assertion. "Society drives us to continually consume, to feed the capitalist hegemony." I don't know about your influences, but I buy iPads because they are cool.

As a medical consumer, you are responsible for your decisions. Don't let anyone—drug company or doctor—talk you into something with which you are uncomfortable. If it doesn't make sense to you, get another opinion or just don't do it. If you see an ad on TV for a facelift that makes you look 20 years younger with a tiny incision, think about it. Does that seem likely?

Our medical decision-making is really an extension of our personal decision-making. To say that the devil made me do it, that our consumerist capitalistic marketing machine made me buy it, that the media influenced me, or that the ubiquitous "society" demanded this or that is simply a cop-out. Owning our bad decisions is core curriculum for the Big Dog degree.

I so want to believe in a Wonder drug, a Wonder lift, a Wonder gizmo that will restore youth and vitality and, as a side effect, result in the absolution of sins. As much as fantasy is fun and fuzzy, good judgment is cold and clear. Maybe in our next life there is an exhibit hall, one that you never have to leave.

Complications

Recently I attended a critical educational meeting titled "TrawlerFest" in Anacortes, Washington. I learned several new skills and procedures, such as changing fuel filters in a diesel engine. It was sort of like sewing an artery, only a little different.

Each morning I walked about two miles to the meeting, a beautiful, raw, Pacific-Northwest stroll along the waterway. On the route was a boatyard, and sitting there, nearly completed, was a brand-new, 91-foot, 10 million-dollar boat. Blue and white, it was a piece of fiberglass sculpture of breathtaking elegance. I chatted up one of workers, who told me it would be launched the day after I left. The commandment about coveting? I violated that one extra large.

Back at home, I received an email from an Anacortes buddy containing a YouTube link. The video showed the boat being lowered into the water on this massive dolly, where it gradually tilted a bit, then lurched to the side, flipped, and sank. I was flabbergasted, to say the least.

This is known as a complication. The boat is a total loss, the company has declared bankruptcy, 70 people have lost their jobs, and apparently the insurance premiums were delinquent.

The first time I see a patient, in fact the very first glimpse, is when I start working to minimize complications. Do I smell cigarette smoke? Do I sense morbid anxiety? Is this person a major whack job? Is there anger or hostility? Does the husband/wife/significant other/whatever do too much of the talking?

The boat-building company has been in and out of business several times. They have four current lawsuits pending. There were liens pending on the engines.

I then assess major risk factors, such as previous healing or infection problems, diabetes, heart or lung disease, or the use of powerful immunosuppressants such as steroids or rheumatoid arthritis drugs.

They had taken a previous boat design and kept adding more layers and equipment to the top part of the boat, and I thought looking at it that it seemed awfully tall for how wide it was.

I won't do six- or seven-hour cosmetic operations. Rarely even four- or five-. Risk goes up with longer cases, so I won't do monster combos. I am a pretty efficient surgeon, a byproduct of the heart surgery days, so I can get a lot done in a few hours, but I've learned not to get greedy.

At the beginning of each surgical case, we run a checklist to make sure we have the right patient, the right procedure, the right everything, essentially.

When they backed the boat into the water, the full-sized door to the engine room, which was on the back of the boat, was open. There were no cables to stabilize the boat in the event of an imbalance.

Of course, I never have complications, but let's say, hypothetically, that I did. Surgeons are human—they like to duck confrontation and awkward situations as much as the next guy. That's exactly the wrong thing to do. If there is a problem, man up (what is the feminine equivalent, by the way?) and own it. Don't blame the patient or the hospital or use any of a universe of lame excuses I've heard in my career. Then, instead of avoiding the patient, you need to see and communicate with them more, rather than less. Some folks I will see every day, or would, if that ever were to happen, which it hasn't, of course.

No one from the boat company can be reached for comment. The insurance companies, the launch contractor, not a word. The only one chirping is the guy who was the project manager, fired last December, because he kept saying they were adding too much weight to the top of the boat.

Surgical complications are often errors in planning, of patient selection, of overreaching, or of faulty judgment. I've noticed that surgeons who have more complications never seem to think it is their fault. Good surgeons look at every adverse outcome critically to determine what they could do better. Good surgeons wrap a patient with a complication in a cocoon of concern and walk them through the tough times.

I could teach you how to do most operations in about half a day. The reason for four years of med school and 10 years of surgical training is so that my patients don't flip over and sink.

We all have screw-ups in our lives, like the time I drove into a low parking garage with a big roof-top carrier. That made a really horrible noise. But nothing tells me more about a person's character than how they handle a bad outcome.

Speaking of character, I know I should not covet a 91-foot boat. I think if it is less than 60 feet, I'm good.

NowCare

Perhaps you ponder the irony that the Affordable Care Act might turbocharge our country's rush to bankruptcy. Perhaps you believe that "ObamaCare" is a necessary response to a health care system that has the coherence of a Sturgis biker rally. Whatever your political, personal, or health care-related proclivities, change is here. Here are some specific strategies for your survival.

Don't be an old, whiny fogey. No one wants to here about how ol' Doc Adams took care of your whole family from cradle to grave and charged you five bucks a visit. Doc Adams didn't have an electronic medical record—he handwrote all of his notes, which no one could read. He may have had all of two years of training after medical school and a bottle of gin in his bottom-right drawer. We current doctors may be soulless, greedy technocrats, but we know a lot and are pretty good. Things have changed for a reason.

Prepare for an overcrowded system. Government-supported health care such as the Veteran's administration, Medicare, Medicaid, and children's health care programs will all expand. The overriding goal of the Affordable Care Act is to expand access, and that will also include private insurance. That's a lot more doctor/clinic visits to a system already pretty saturated.

So you need to get your game face on. Be really sure you need to see a provider in the first place. One of the ways insurance becomes "affordable" is by massively jacking up deductibles. Thus, many visits are on your dime. Be sure you need it.

Go well prepared. Have your med lists, referral documents, implant cards—anything pertinent—ready to go. Don't show up for a blood pressure visit and not know your blood pressure trends. Try to limit your visit to one or two problems, or you run the risk of getting blown off. Many offices ask you to fill out online histories before you go. No one wants to hear about how you are too old or traditional to use a computer. Don't annoy someone who might help you. Just get with it.

Look out for yourself. Don't assume that laboratory, x-ray, or pathology reports are always reviewed. We've all heard stories about Uncle Eddie's lung tumor that was there on an x-ray two years before he started coughing up blood. If you have a test, make a follow-up call if you don't hear the results. Don't assume your mammogram is normal just because you didn't hear. When things get busy, important findings can be missed.

Be a pest if things aren't happening. If a referral, test, or procedure has been suggested, stay after it. Fortunately, my staff compensates for Dr. Space Case and pesters me.

Don't get sick. It is disingenuous to complain about your lousy luck and the ruinous cost of care when you are packing 60 extra pounds and smoke a pack a day. Or maybe you are some stringy yuppie who keeps cracking collarbones on your extreme mountain bike. That 19,000-dollar plate job sucks up a lot of premiums.

Be patient. Service will be less personal and more digital, and you will have to put up with seeing lots of different doctors or physician assistants. The future is about systems and not about individual providers. Rather than being a Doc Adams patient, you will be a HealthCo client.

Despite this somewhat dystopian view, I see a powerfully positive angle. If all this care is indifferently pixilated, who looks after us? We do. Our families do.

So many of our maladies are stress-related, nutrition-related, or condition-related. We are anxious, sedentary consumers of junk. I think sometimes we confuse natural remedies with tie-dyed funky herbs sprinkled over free-range organic chickens that received bereavement counseling before being beheaded.

You know most of the natural remedies. It is now strongly in your financial interest to try them out.

Rather than rail at Washington about our health care, let's take a frank look at our own responsibility. Insurance, Medicare, or whatever is for when we have lousy luck or genes or just wear out. The rest of our health—really our wellness—is within our control.

There aren't a lot of happy victims. I have the privilege to interact with persons who bear great suffering with equanimity, who express gratitude when I see no redeemable features in their life. The new age of health care represents a transition from the paternalistic omniscience of Doc Adams to the self-actualized, self-responsible consumer.

Of course I don't like the Affordable Care Act. It doesn't cover cosmetic surgery. What were they thinking?

The List

Everyone hates being left out.

Maybe you remember, as a kid, everyone talking about a birthday party to which you weren't invited. Perhaps that list with the final roster of the basketball team didn't include your name.

Imagine, then, my feelings when Medicare published the list of 4,000 doctors who were paid over a million dollars in Medicare reimbursement. Not only did I not make that list, I wasn't even on the *Montana* list.

Imagine, too, my poor mother, sitting in the dining room at the Springs in Missoula, listening to another lady prattle on about her grandson the dermatologist who did make the list. The humiliation.

If there is a list that involves big bucks, I want to be on it.

There is little doubt as to why Medicare released that data. The federal government wants to magnanimously expand health care, but doesn't want to increase already massive deficits. Every year they cut reimbursement to hospitals and physicians to accommodate the growing number of beneficiaries.

If they publish numbers that suggest doctors are getting rich on Medicare, then no one will care if reimbursement is cut even further.

What the articles did not say was that many physicians, such as oncologists or rheumatologists, purchase drugs (many of which are fabulously expensive) or other supplies and administer them in their office. They then bill Medicare for the drugs or supplies. As a result, it looks like all this money is going into the pocket of the doctor. With a smirk on its smarmy little bureaucratic face, Medicare then watches the public turn on the doctors. When the vote comes up for another round of cuts, Medicare has a ready-made mob.

Medicare reimbursement, believe it or not, is really lousy. One patient of mine had a large skin cancer on his face that required a complex reconstruction. He noted that on the back cover of my book I was holding an old rental chainsaw as a prop. "I saw what Medicare paid you for all that surgery. It was pitiful." So he bought me a new chainsaw. You wouldn't think a chainsaw would choke you up, but it can.

Doctors are not blameless. The response to lower reimbursement per procedure is often to increase the volume of procedures. We do way more hips, knees, cataracts, coronary bypasses, breast reductions—you name it—than any other country. Doctors work harder if they make more money.

Well, that's terrible, you say—medical decisions should have nothing to do with getting paid.

It's not that simple. Let's say your hip hurts. The Utopian National Health Service in, say, Canada or Norway, tells you that you aren't going to die from hip pain. Take a little ibuprofen and live with it. "But I want to ski!" you cry. In this country it is off to the OR for a titanium hip, and you're on the slopes in a few months. Is that unnecessary surgery? Depends. If it is your hip—yes. My hip—no.

Another example: You are a 75-year-old with advanced cancer. The statistics say you're cooked. For a $125,000 course of chemo and radiation you might get another six months or a year, two on the outside. Our Utopian NHS would say, "You've had a nice life, deal with it." In this country, people say, "Hit me with your best shot."

Here are the basic issues. We all think we should decrease our collective health care utilization, with the exception being my hip or cataract or chemo.

For the most part, we are spending money that is not ours. Watch how people eat on a cruise ship, where the food is "all you can wolf down."

"But I paid into Medicare for 30 years," you say. Right. Halfway through the first of your three joint replacements, you burned all that and more.

We can't possibly have a meaningful discussion on health care because politicians pander to their constituencies about their "right to health care." Can you imagine a Senate candidate saying he/she will slash Medicare spending by making affluent recipients pay for their own hips?

The solution? Health care has to come down to economic earth. Much of elective surgery should probably come out of Medicare and go onto the open market. Medicare should cover basic, proven medical care. If you want the latest zillion-dollar drug, or if you want to go to the ICU when you are demented and have pneumonia, then you will have to pay for it. Your children will yank that plug right out of the wall.

Death Squads? For sure. It makes no sense to me to spend billions on futile care, often for people who did nothing but abuse their bodies, and not properly educate our children or maintain civil infrastructure. By not making decisions, we are making terrible decisions.

I know why I wasn't on the list. Medicare doesn't count chainsaws.

Watch Out

Watch out. Someone in your family may be trying to kill you.

Most of us who take care of trauma patients expect a few shootings and stabbings around the holiday that are inflicted by "loved ones."

Detectives in a murder case usually don't have to look much further than the spouse or main squeeze of the deceased to find their perp.

That doesn't happen in my family, of course. Before our holiday gatherings, I call to remind my sister-in-law to lock up my brother's AR-15 assault rifle and his Glock 9mm. I can't say everyone is thrilled with the plastic utensils or the sparkling cider, but at least the local cops aren't regulars at dinner anymore.

The least of your worries are the guns and knives. The biggest threat from your relatives is something you can't even see.

Genes.

I saw a patient recently whose aunt had died of breast cancer, and both her mother and sister had been treated with surgery and radiation for breast cancer. My patient had tested positive for the BRCA gene, which gave her a 60% likelihood of getting breast cancer herself. She has chosen to have bilateral mastectomies with reconstruction.

Generally I am not a big believer in luck. Sure, you make a lot of your own luck with perseverance, hard work, and draconian self-denial. Not true with genetics. Show me the "self-made" man who built his own chromosomes.

I've been reasonably lucky with my genetic hand. Our clan has premature coronary disease, but they tend not to die of it. I am blessed with average looks, which is good, because if you are too pretty people can act weird around you. I have enough intelligence to do my job, but by not being overly bright, I've had to learn how to hustle. In my case, the hair loss is due not to genetics but rather to an excess of a particularly potent form of testosterone.

Some folks aren't as fortunate. Members of some families get one little coronary blockage in the wrong place and they all drop dead. Other families grow cancers like weeds. There are an endless number of genetic diseases that involve the absence of an enzyme, resulting in catastrophic metabolic squalls.

On a lesser scale, you can also inherit saggy necks or vexatious love handles, which are good for my business.

Watch out for your family members. Just because my family has gone to metal detectors at Thanksgiving doesn't mean we don't love and trust each other. Nothing wrong with checking.

Make a chart of you and your family. If you don't remember genetics class, flunked it, or attended it impaired, get a family tree from some online source.

I asked one guy if he had anything significant in his family history. "My wife has diabetes." While your spouse certainly can lead to your premature death, it will not be from genetic causes.

Anyway, look first at first-degree relatives. That means mom, dad, sister, brother, or your kids. Second-degree relatives like grandparents or aunts/uncles count, too, but not as much. What conditions do they have, what was the cause of their death?

If your father and brother have high cholesterol, are hypertensive, and maybe have had a heart attack or two, do you think you are somehow immune? Get your lipids checked, watch your blood pressure, and ask your provider about a stress test. Otherwise, it might be toes up for you.

Pay attention to breast, ovarian, and colon cancer. They are often related and have a heavy genetic component. Don't blow off those colonoscopies or mammograms unless you want to be the next "X" on the family tree.

I attend tumor boards at two local hospitals, and at each we have genetic counselors who provide insights into the growing fund of knowledge regarding cancer genetics. What is remarkable is how often we discuss advanced cancer cases in patients who had a very obvious, and had obviously ignored, family history.

As we move toward nationalized/socialized health care, it will be more important than ever to look out for yourself. If some illness seems to be popping up a lot in your close relatives, get screened for it. Do not expect your providers to think of everything. They will be too busy looking up all the side effects of their own anti-depressants.

Our greatest blessings, and sometimes our greatest sorrows, arise from family. We are stuck with our genes, just as we are inextricably entwined with our relatives.

There within, however, lie choices. If our natural family is estranged or diminished by circumstance, our adjunct families become paramount. We have families in the workplace, on a team, in a church, or in any collaborative endeavor. If we give generously of our heart to others, perhaps it will be filled in return, leaving loneliness looking elsewhere.

Maybe I'll take just a little bottle of pepper spray to Christmas dinner. You never know with family.

Locked Out

Here is how you get in trouble:

I usually leave my keys in the car, in the garage, so that if I have to go busting out at night to the hospital I am not frantically tearing the house apart looking for them.

But I had to leave the car on the street because the roof guys were parked in the driveway. As usual, I left the keys in car, but also locked it.

I came back outside, found the car locked, and after tearing the house apart, found the spare.

I went back to the hospital for a late case, a sweet little eyelid repair, and on the way out I searched my white coat, ever so desperately, for the spare key. Which was sitting on the center console of the locked car. But, I always have a spare taped under the chassis, which I remembered I had used a few weeks ago and had really meant to replace but hadn't.

Three keys. All locked in the car.

I called a lock guy, at 5:00 P.M. on Friday, who was helping another moron, but could come in 40 minutes. Fortunately, the weather was nice while I sat outside reflecting on my missteps.

Lock Guy showed up in an old Toyota mini-truck, which looked like it had been used in a Baghdad firefight. His straining t-shirt, of similar vintage as the truck, bore evidence of many vehicular encounters.

Affably, he quickly appraised the situation. He inserted a very fine wedge between the door and frame, and then gently tapped it until there was an appreciable gap. He then slid an inflatable bladder, like a blood pressure cuff, into the opening, and insufflated it until the opening would admit his tools.

He had a series of long, magnetized instruments, which he used to approach the door handles and lock buttons. It was very much like watching a laparoscopic gall bladder removal.

After no success with the locks and handles, he noticed one of the several spare keys. After a mildly speculative glance at me, he snaked his device across to the center console, and adroitly snagged a key. With a feather touch, he delivered the key through the door.

"40 bucks," he said cheerfully. I gave him 50.

I always try to learn from my complications. What could I have done better?

40

First of all, if you are departing from a routine, note that and make a plan. For instance, I always use a triple antibiotic irrigation when placing any type of implant for reconstruction. It may be, though, that the patient has an allergy to one of those antibiotics. When things are outside the ordinary, you really need to pay attention. It always seems to be the carpenters with 30 years of experience who cut their fingers off.

I also learned that there are a lot of really talented people out there. Cabinetmakers, tailors, bakers, auto-body guys, and many other artisans possess an amazing degree of technical skill—steady hands, great dexterity, and nimble minds. Surgeons are often celebrated for their skill, largely because most of us fear illness, and surgery is a bit of a dark art. I obviously have no problem with that, but there are a lot of operators out there, like my Lock Guy, whose greatness is both daily and obscure.

The most potent message in this incident for me was the recognition of my extraordinary privilege. I have an intensely interesting job (also intensely annoying at times, but whose job isn't?) for which I am highly compensated. I have worked fiercely since junior high to get where I am and to stay where I am, but a lot of people work hard.

The difference-maker for me was being born to two well educated parents, going to good schools, and having all kinds of people tell me I was bright and talented and I would someday be a terrific surgeon. Other than taking hundreds of nasty courses and taking eight million tests over the last 45 years, I haven't had a single obstacle to overcome. Healthy, white, male, two great parents, supportive wife and family, United States, Montana—no excuses.

Humility comes not just from standing there helplessly in your little doctor suit in a parking lot next to your locked car, waiting to be saved by the Lock Guy.

It comes from knowing that virtually none of us are self-made. If you start thinking that yeah, I be pretty bad, pretty slick, I am the Man—well, let's stick you as one of eight kids in south Sudan and see how well you do. You'd be locked out. When Lock Guy opened the door of that car, somehow a flood of gratitude was unlocked in me. It is good to be needed, and just as good to need others.

I think I will have all the windows removed in my car. Maybe the fresh air will snap me out of it.

3) INSIDE THE LINES

Medicine by nature is a very personal business. Illness or injury is very intrusive—not only do you have to deal with the injured limb or the shortness of breath, you have to divulge practically your whole life to the system caring for you. Even a routine visit means you answer every conceivable question from your medications to whether someone is beating you up at home.

These articles are of a personal nature, dealing with everything from sexual behavior (and misbehavior) to grief and loss. Insights gained from caring for thousands of patients over the years seem to have a common theme: We all tend to share the same hopes and dreams and strengths and sins. We are what we are, and we ain't what we ain't.

PoliPorn

Just when you think there can't possibly be any more high-level sexual malfeasance, a whole new cycle erupts. The ironically named Anthony Weiner, a former congressman banished for "sexting" photographs of, based on his behavior, his brains—is running for mayor of New York. Rather astonishingly, having been previously disgraced, he did not forbear his multimedia communication. Even more remarkable is the presence of his ever-stoical wife at yet another confessional press conference.

Certainly, though, in all fairness, my devoted wife would be at my side, as well. Except that she would be standing stoically while my closed refurbished casket was lowered into a hole, likely just south of the landfill.

Eliot Spitzer, former governor of New York, former customer of prostitutes specializing in role-playing, is running for comptroller of New York, whatever that is. Then there is good ol' Silvio Berlusconi of Italy, with his underage girl problem, the reliable Dominique Strauss Kahn of France "pimping" fame, and the recent adventures of the mayor of San Diego. These guys keep popping up in sequels of their own bad movies.

Then there is the litany of abuses by clergy, by coach figures such as in the Penn State tragedies, and in our own region, as well. Famous athletes, a president—basically everywhere and everyone is acting up.

It seems to me that we really don't have a clear understanding of ourselves as sexual beings. In some cases we are taught that sex is sinful and grimy, which then paradoxically creates a repressive urge that explodes in inappropriate behavior—witness the fallen clergy and sanctimonious politicians of all faiths. In other cases there is the "if it feels good, do it" mentality, which results in irresponsible baby-making and disease transmission, as well as sexual objectification, usually of women. Certainly I have been repeatedly subjected to treatment as merely an object of raw physical lust, and, well, I mean, it could happen.

Sexual behavior has an enormous impact on the social structure. Once I croak and have my exit interview with the Almighty, which hopefully will go well, as long as He doesn't have access to certain video replay, I am going to ask Him, in His infinite wisdom, why He ever, ever coupled(!) the act of sexual intercourse with human reproduction. (I use the pronoun He intentionally—no woman would have done that.) The gravest, most significant act in life is to create another person. Certainly the most expensive and aggravating. So here is the heaviest responsibility in life, and how is it achieved? An irrepressible, visceral urge, fueled by a couple of drinks, a grunting exchange of bodily fluids between persons who may or may not be well acquainted, and—boom—a new person. In my estimation, that is nuts. That's like eating a brownie and ending up with a house payment.

Look at the social havoc of sexual carelessness. A huge percentage of persons in prison were unwanted, neglected, or abused as children. It is difficult to find a social problem, whether it is poverty, environmental stress due to overpopulation, or crime, that isn't related to unplanned, poorly supported, poorly nourished, and poorly educated children. The social and economic costs of sexually transmitted disease are staggering, as well.

This is not some sanctimonious plea for a puritanical revival. That would result in us all consorting with prostitutes who dress up like Little Bo Peep while we wear sheep costumes. Rather I think we need to start taking the business of our personal behaviors very seriously or our social structure is going to fall apart. I don't care who or what or how you express your sexuality—none of my business. But never force your desires on another person, especially one who is incapable of consent. Don't promise fidelity on an altar and then text a picture of your sorry anatomy to someone named Stormy. Don't throw kids in the world you aren't ready for and can't support. Don't hook up with whomever and then expect Medicaid to fork out for your expensive infection.

We can see ourselves as moral, or religious, or not. But we must see ourselves as the animals, basically, that we are. We have biological urges to eat, to sleep, to eliminate, and to procreate. Of course we are not animals—animals at least take a sexual break for most of the year, while we are 24/7/365. We cannot believe we are too moral, or disciplined, or too intellectually armored to avoid behaving badly.

Sexual intimacy is the most sublime human experience. Even better than a new 54-foot trawler yacht with active stabilizers. Perhaps its sublimity comes from its simplicity—its deep biological, ancient imperative. But therein lies the danger: Its primitive power can overwhelm us and irrevocably change our lives.

I always thought I would run for political office, but I don't know now. I may not have what it takes. Does yacht porn count?

Judgment

You never know what might be just around the corner.

I had just passed through a narrow spot between two islands in British Columbia, having timed the transit so that the huge tides in the area wouldn't throw me up on the rocks. My plan was to tie up in Maple Bay, a cozy marina protected from the various gales and hurricanes that had coincidentally chosen the same week I had to play in the Pacific Northwest.

My relief at getting through the Narrows was short lived—there was a "Youth Sailing Regatta" in the bay, and at least 30 colorful sailing rigs were zipping around, more or less randomly, in the small bay. I slowed to a crawl, much less than the 5 mph speed limit posted on a floating buoy at the entrance.

I had just about made it through this minefield when I saw that some poor young guy had lost control of his sailboat. The lines had slipped from his hands, and a gust of wind had filled the sail. He was careening directly toward the side of my boat.

This was bad for several reasons. A collision with a 60-foot, 50-ton boat would likely render both his body and his sailboat a buffet for the local sea creatures. From my standpoint, a big fiberglass divot would greatly displease John, the owner of my boat, a kind gentleman (smarter certainly, than I, and a couple of rungs higher on the food chain) who allows me to rent his boat a few days a year, with the proviso that I don't knock holes in it.

I looked ahead to make sure there was no oncoming traffic, just another sailboat well off to the right (starboard, if you are cool), and gunned the engine to avoid the impending collision with the hapless sailboat on the port side. He just missed me.

Of course the guy on the right saw none of this, just saw a big powerboat going too fast in the bay, and as we crossed he gestured obscenely, and shouted the most ill-mannered and ungracious invective.

I am used to being verbally abused, having spent a considerable amount of my life in the ER in the presence of those with inadequate liquor management skills. I've been a recipient of similar gestures while driving, and in some cases have deserved the reprimand.

It was the sheer injustice of the situation that bothered me. I made a heroic effort to save some errant sailor, and I get trashed for it.

Of course, the sanctimonious sailor on the starboard had no idea why I was speeding or what the situation was.

But how often have I done that?

I once became so frustrated with a grumpy and difficult patient with a wound on her leg that I told her that I didn't think I could deal with her attitude anymore, that she should find another doctor. She suddenly dissolved into tears, telling me that she had promised her husband he could die at home from his terminal intestinal cancer, but that his constant vomiting was close to finishing her as well.

Another patient consistently missed or was late to appointments, and when we mentioned how difficult this was on our schedule, she told us about her son with a traumatic brain injury. He really couldn't be left alone due to severe mood swings and violent behavior, and, on top of that, he had to be in court frequently as a result of the above.

I have to be very careful in cosmetic surgery—is a patient's request for alteration of their nose simply because they busted it in a volleyball game, or does it represent a deep sense of self-loathing? Does a 25-year-old woman want a breast augmentation because she would like a more proportioned figure, or is it because she is trying to hang on to a boyfriend with a Hooters fixation?

I need to know the whole story—port and starboard. Does a patient take medications that impair healing or cause bleeding? Is this patient a head case? Should I ignore poorly controlled diabetes or smoking because I want to fill my schedule? Have I carefully studied the previous op reports, so that neither my patient nor I end up with a big hole at the waterline?

There are certainly Biblical admonitions about judgment. I think it is extending them to the medical, nautical, and personal daily situations that is difficult.

I know what I am going to do. I am going to ask John if we can install a water cannon on the boat, so that the next time someone waves their finger at me or swears at me I can blast them into Puget Sound.

It's probably too late for me to become a better person.

Envy

The moment I stepped on the dock I saw her. I'd seen her before, but had known that her perfect curves and dramatic lines would never be mine. Perhaps a bit heavy at 123,000 pounds, but still....

The owner, Vince, was standing on the dock conversing with Mike, who owned the adjacent and equally stunning 63-foot trawler yacht in the next slip. Both were early- to mid-60s, very casually but expensively dressed. I intruded into their conversation.

Both were semi-retired, their business interests generally self-sustaining, and they were touring the San Juan and Gulf Islands before venturing northward to the British Columbia coast.

They politely inquired about the vessel on which I had arrived. I turned and pointed to the boat I had chartered. I don't whether it was the light or the position at the dock, but it suddenly it looked like a rusted-out 1983 Volkswagen Rabbit. The two men politely avoided comment.

I was suffused with envy. Cruising around on 1.6-million-dollar luxury homes while your "business interests" continued to make donkey carts full of money.

The back door of Mike's boat opened and a four-year-old, dark-haired cutie accosted us: "It's time for breakfast!"

"Guess I'd better go," said Mike.

"Is that your granddaughter?" Vince asked.

"Well," Mike replied, "sort of."

Sort of?

"My son died in a motorcycle crash and I've adopted her."

"Wow," said Vince. "I know how that feels. We lost our daughter four years ago to a seizure disorder. She aspirated and died during the night. Twenty years old."

I returned to my suddenly less dumpy charter boat, with my wife and night-shift-grumpy but oh-so-alive daughter, and my envy dissipated, replaced with an embarrassed gratitude.

Although I'm a surgeon, I've always tried to deal with my patients as dimensional beings. Fixing parts is not always healing. Sometimes I must address the emotional and spiritual aspects of a wound that may be deeper than that of the flesh.

I've learned that we know little of most people's inner lives. We assume that because of their possessions or homes or jobs or their cheery demeanor that their lives are smooth and uncomplicated.

We assume that because they have a new 58-footer with a full-height engine room, state-of-the-art Simrad autopilot, and a fully enclosed fly bridge, while a business prints money that life couldn't be better.

We don't know that a person will be attending parent-teacher conferences at the age of 70. We don't know that every time Vince and his wife go to a wedding of a friend's daughter, they are reminded that their daughter will never be married or give them grandchildren.

We don't know anything, really, about most of the people in our lives, yet we assume so much.

I can't discount the possibility that this episode represented some sort of celestial smack-down of my sinful nature. After all, envy is one of the seven deadly sins, and the tenth commandment addresses coveting thy neighbor's wife and such.

I see a few "trophy wives" on the docks. When I think of younger wives, I don't think of steamy romps with nubile young sylphs. I think of big credit card bills. I don't covet big credit card bills. That's not a gender bash, by the way. Boy-toys like credit cards, too, just so you aspiring cougars know.

The real risk of envy is that it blocks our gratitude receptors. (I don't know if gratitude receptors actually exist, but if they don't, they should). Gratitude research is actually a very hot topic now in psychological circles. Expression of gratitude has been linked to improved sleep, decreased anxiety and depression, and improved romantic relationships. The lesson is that even if your chartered boat looks like a rusted-out 1983 VW Rabbit, be grateful, for that and the treasures within. Be grateful that you don't bear the burdens of those you might envy.

I am going to have to see a specialist, I guess—a theological consultant. I don't covet my neighbor's wife, his servants, his ox, or his donkey. Just his boat. Remember that those commandments were written way long ago, long before flat-screen TVs and fiberglass trawlers. Don't think Moses didn't chuck a few of those commandments on the way down the hill, pertaining to his particular issues.

Surely those rules don't apply to me.

Broken

After my second year of general surgery training, back in the Hoover administration, I spent a year working in a surgical laboratory. My focus was in organ preservation, and many hapless pigs underwent heart-lung transplants so I could bolster my academic credentials.

Since I didn't have to take call and do clinical work, I had a job moonlighting at night in a local ER near Salt Lake City. I made the first real money of my life, and in a frenzy of consumerist lust, I proceeded to blow it, big time.

I bought a starter home, as well as a sporty new car. My moment of triumph came when I pulled into the rather steeply sloped driveway of my new house in my new car. Of course, being the stick-shift stud I was, I got out of the car and forgot to set the brake. The car rolled down the driveway, the driver's-side door swinging wildly, and the car did an elegant pirouette. The also-new mailbox sliced off the car door before it was destroyed, and the graceful arc continued onto the newly sodded lawn, which was also desecrated before the car came to rest upon a rather pricey and now bisected maple tree.

I once hooked up a boat trailer to a Suburban and failed to properly engage the hitch. The nose of the boat ended up just behind the driver's seat.

I have dropped a sizeable bottle of maple syrup on a Persian rug.

I am capable of supreme concentration in the operating room, for any period of time necessary. I am similarly focused when operating a car or a charter boat. A $10,000 deposit will do that to you. But if I have a bowl of spaghetti sauce over a clean floor, watch out.

I guess breaking things has caused me to reflect on brokenness.

I've seen a lot of that lately. One guy rolled his car off an icy highway and managed to spear his forehead as well as upper and lower lids with a metal fencepost. I've seen two bad cases of frozen fingers and feet just recently. I've seen broken ears, noses, jaws, and sternums. I've been reconstructing a disturbing number of missing breasts due to cancer.

There is a lot of brokenness in our lives. There can be broken promises, broken relationships, broken dreams. Sometimes our bodies are broken.

Very often physical brokenness comes from a deeper spiritual brokenness. Addictions such as alcohol, methamphetamine, or nicotine come from that deep spiritual well of despair, bubbling up until the body is broken. Another viciously toxic substance is loneliness.

Any health care provider who ignores a patient's spiritual or psychological state will at best patch the superficial cracks, ignoring the deeper underlying cry for help.

Today is Christmas. Regardless of your religious faith, your indifference, or deliberate agnosticism, Christmas is a time for spiritual inventory. It is a light in the darkness, a star in the night, an offer of redemption. It is recognition that we are human, and thus broken at times.

It is also a mandate, a responsibility. I have done three surgical residencies, am certified by three boards of surgery, and by far the most important thing I do is listen. I envelop a quivering hand in mine and say nothing.

Christmas this year means that you understand that this is a broken world and you yourself are broken at times. More importantly, it means that you must embrace the role of healer.

The most meaningful thing you can ever do in life is relieve the suffering of others. Are you seeking meaning in your life? That's it.

Do you know those who are broken? Of course you do. Maybe you can't remove a brain tumor or rebuild a breast, but you can restore hope to a broken person. If a baby lying in a cowshed 2,000 years ago could do it, so can you.

It doesn't matter if you lay brick or teach school or drive truck. The most potent aspect of healing is within your power. It is the ability to get outside yourself and sense the need in those around you. It is incredibly hard, and yet so simple.

Sometimes all we need in those dark nights of the soul is a little affirmation, a listening ear, a light. The Star of Bethlehem means that those who are heavy laden might have some rest.

If you see a soul burdened, extend a hand.

If you see me pulling a cake out of the oven, run for your life.

Running Away

Speaking of running away...

One day recently I worked with three different surgeons on cancer removal and reconstructive procedures. I feel proud of the surgical oncology programs where I work, infused as they are with great young talent. Some specialties we can't recruit/retain for love or (lots of) money, but general surgery has a bright future.

Each of these surgeons related a frustrating story. One had seen a patient in the office for a large abdominal hernia. He had suggested that the patient's uncontrolled diabetes, cigarette smoking, and morbid obesity might be addressed prior to a surgical repair. The patient had somehow heard "you are a lazy, addicted, lard bottom" and had called the department to complain.

Another surgeon had done an elegant laparoscopic procedure on a high-risk patient, only to have a clip come off a blood vessel in the middle of the night. A third had done a stomach resection, and the patient had developed a leak in the connection of the ends.

"Maybe I will move to Fernie, British Columbia, and do only gall bladders," mused one surgeon. We were each thinking of ways to run away—to find a cozy place somewhere over the rainbow without leakage, bleeding, or angry patients.

I was thinking of a community college in Anacortes, WA, where I could do a course in marine diesel technology. Never seen a diesel engine get infected.

I thought, after 12 years of medical school and residency, that life would smooth out and quiet down and would be a chill, moneyed cruise. Instead, when I realized I was now primarily responsible for the patients, my anxiety level found a higher frequency.

I thought once my kids weren't toddling and trying to kill themselves constantly, that knot in my chest would soften, but then came cars and adolescent anguish. Once they were 21, maybe—but then there were tumors and organic chemistry and unsatisfactory boyfriends.

My daughter Cathy has started a master's degree in social work and counseling, and mentioned that people with a diagnosis of depression often have difficulty with new or stressful situations. We had an interesting discussion—is stress abnormal? Is disappointment a diagnosis? Is sadness a sickness?

I have made the startling realization, at the age of 58, that I will never board the cruise ship of utter contentment. It doesn't dock where I have chosen to live.

Of course, you already know that, and are probably wondering how such a slow learner holds a medical license.

Consistent happiness and contentment in our lives is not a realistic expectation. Especially if we expect it. What is reasonable?

If you do surgery, teach kids, coach a team, run a business, or put it out there in any fashion, you are going to take some shots. You will have bad results that aren't your fault, but will get blamed roundly for them.

But if you sit home in the dark playing video games, you don't make any money, you miss the winning shot, and will probably overdose on Cheetos. No risk, no rush.

Happiness tends to come in brief, intense pulses—often unexpected, elegant little moments. While recognizing that we are not entitled to all-we-can-eat joy is important, it is more critical to have the facility to see the ephemeral victories for which we live, the victories that never happen if we run away.

One of those cases last week was a double breast reconstruction, which I think turned out beautifully—good size, nice shape, just like the real deal, only perkier. The patient was less impressed, saying, "I thought I would look more like the girls at Hooters."

I've learned my lesson. When I finish with that diesel engine, it will be a double-D.

Coyote Love

Perhaps the best way to convey the quality of my singing voice is for you to envision a coyote with an acute bowel obstruction. Tenors, however, are in short supply, as in the process of aging men tend to acquire deeper voices and become baritones or basses. They also tend to become more mature, reflective, and responsible. None of these things have happened to me, however, and thus my participation in the Billings Symphony Chorale and Vivaldi's "Gloria."

Our director, Dr. Steven Hart, exhorts us to enunciate, express, and artistically render the notes and words of the maestros, rather than shower-stall bellering. It is "glow-ree-aah" rather than "gluriah" when singing "Gloria." Vince Lombardi coaching on the Senior Circuit.

It is no secret that the classical musical audience is, well, of a certain age. It is quite possible that if we sang "hippopotamus" instead of "glow-ree-aah" the audience wouldn't hear the difference. The younger listeners wouldn't either, because their hearing has been blasted away by artillery-level sound pressure from their iPods and earphones.

But maybe there are two or three other choral directors listening in the St. Patrick's Cathedral, and they will know. And most importantly, Dr. Hart tells us, we will know. We cannot honor the astonishing beauty of the work, ourselves, and each other if we do not do our best.

The late Steve Jobs, in the early development of the Macintosh computer, made his engineers redesign a circuit board because it looked cluttered. "Steve, Dude," they pleaded, "it all goes inside a box. No one will see it. No one will care." Jobs replied, "If a device isn't elegant all the way through, even unseen, it cannot function elegantly."

I had a pediatric surgery professor who would freak out if all the suture ends weren't of the same length, or if you tore tape to put on a dressing instead of cutting it neatly with a scissors. "This is someone's *baby*," he'd sputter. "What will the mom think about your work inside?" Playing the baby card is always a cheap shot.

We finished our new facility last December, and after six months we became eligible to be accredited by the American Association for Accreditation of Ambulatory Surgical Facilities, or AAAASF. You don't have to be accredited to do surgery in a facility, remarkably—all you need is a medical license (it doesn't have to be in the specialty) and the ability to talk people into having surgery in your garage or RV or whatever. But being the hopelessly conventional, boring guys and gals we are, we thought it would be good to be inspected and accredited.

Many of you, probably most of you, have been inspected by someone at sometime—health department, fire department, hospital inspections (nasty), auditors, whatever. It's like a 14-foot colonoscopy. We had to have hundreds of pages of policies ("Do you have a policy stating your procedure in the event of a Martian invasion?"), and they inspect the facility ("I see you have a men's room and a women's room, what about a restroom for your transgender patients?") What's frustrating about an inspection is that you prepare for months, all this stuff, and then they check about five percent of it, with artfully written policies pertaining to terrorist attacks on the coffee machine unread.

We passed, gratefully, the prospect of doing it again too terrible to contemplate. And, I rather imagine, another three years will go by before the next inspection, and not a patient will ask us if we are an accredited facility. But we will know. Glow-ree-aah.

Excellence is a very private matter. In my cardiac surgery training, I worked with my chairman on a guy who'd blown an ascending aortic aneurysm. We ground it out for eight hours, finishing up about 3:00 A.M., the guy snatched out of the Big Drain to live another couple decades. We walked out of the OR to an empty, silent hallway. "Boah," he said to me in his thick Arkansas accent, "theah ought to be a hunnert thousand people on theah feet cheering us right now, for what we've done. And heah we are, alone. I guess the Lawd knows."

It is only in the supreme privacy of our minds, those closets of the soul that no one else enters, that we know if we have done our best. Sure, we took out the defensive end, but could we also have blown up the safety and sprung the running back for a touchdown? As long as we're getting existential here, if our actions define our existence, is not our effort the very definition of ourselves? If the proper treatment of Vivaldi's work honors his genius, does not our attitude of excellence and an assiduous approach to our work serve as a statement of who we are, and an appreciation of the gifts we have been given?

Well, maybe one of those gifts is not vocal brilliance. But I can probably help that poor coyote with the bowel obstruction.

Mentors

One of my first medical mentors was a cardiologist who, starting when I was in high school and extending over the years into medical school, allowed me to "shadow" him. Dr. Stone is the epitome of the gentleman physician: bright, erudite, skilled, but most of all, kind. He taught me that no matter how quick your brain or hot your hands, if you couldn't care for people, do something else.

Somewhere during those years my hometown hospital started a heart surgery program, and when the surgeon arrived in a red Turbo Carrera with a smoking blonde girlfriend, a slightly different role model emerged. If you were to say I was chasing money and glamour, you would be right.

I always thought I would be an academic surgeon, a professor making great advances and teaching younger surgeons. I spent a total of 10 years in surgical training, and for the most part the professors were treacherous, whiny, backstabbing, venal, rapacious, and, mostly, small characters. Several of them were world leaders, innovators, and towering figures in their fields. I wouldn't let any of them babysit my pet rattlesnake.

I just didn't want to be like the professors. I discovered that the guys in private practice were calm, slick, personable, and weren't always acting like they were getting ready to take a shower in a maximum-security prison.

A wonderful man named Steve Hubbard, along with my other senior partner Tim Dernbach, guided me through my early years of heart surgery in Billings. These guys were so good that they could fix anything I could screw up, telling me all along how good I was. They could operate circles around the professors, and made a lot more money, because there wasn't a long row of non-productive academic hogs at the trough.

When the heart surgery world began to shrink away, a hoops buddy named Walt Peet, a local plastic surgeon, told me to consider retraining. Walt is another elegant surgeon, never any fuss, the ever-deft bedside manner—you just want to be like him. He directed me to a deeply satisfying surgical rebirth.

When I returned from yet another tumultuous turn in academia, I joined Walt's partner Steve Grosso in practice. Steve mentored the start of my plastic surgical career, and like other great surgeons, manages to make things seem obvious and uncomplicated.

The most essential mentors, of course, are our parents. I hit the cosmic lottery with Bess and Al. Ever loving, temperate, educated, disciplined, fun—I haven't a single childhood trauma or excuse.

Most real medical education occurs outside the classroom. When the bullets start flying, it is the person next to you that really matters. How do they react? How do they solve problems? How do they comport themselves?

Mentoring is certainly not unique to medicine—it occurs in every walk of life. Even computer hackers and drug dealers have to learn from someone.

A lot of those academic surgeons did very little mentoring because they were afraid of being usurped. A good mentor has to have a deep sense of personal security. Helping someone else to get better means you had better keep getting better yourself. Big dogs are cool with that. Little dogs bite you on the ankle.

Remember that when you are teaching, your pupils are watching everything. I observed my surgical teachers operate, of course, but I looked at their interactions with staff and patients, their fitness, cars, houses, clothes, marriages, and children.

I listened to an interview recently with Bill Parcells, a pro football Hall of Fame and Super Bowl-winning coach. Asked about any regrets, he said, "I was a lousy parent." See, that's a deal killer for me. I honestly can't think of one person I truly admire who is a lousy parent.

In the recent *Gazette* "40 under 40" feature, Dr. Barry McKenzie mentioned how influential his senior partner had been. Dr. Dennis Maier just showed Barry and the rest of us that calm and reason and right work most of the time. Denny, whose next mission is coaching Legion baseball, Lord help him (consider brain MRI), wastes no time fussing about the dissolution of younger surgeons or players. He just shows them how to do it right, and because it's him, they believe him.

The most meaningful thing we ever do in life is to relieve the suffering of another, to raise another person through loving intervention. Think of the anxiety you felt when you were new and inexperienced; think of those who pulled you onto the raft when you were drowning. Now hold out your hand.

I hope to see Dr. Stone this weekend in Missoula, after all these years. I will pick him up in a blue Honda.

Loser

I have never been a good loser.

We are taught to be gracious in defeat, to shake hands and congratulate, to display character in adversity. I was taught that. Didn't stick.

At a college track meet in Missoula decades ago, I was just about to pass this dude from Idaho State at the finish line when his teammate behind me just grabbed my shirt. Denied the victory, I turned around and unleashed a stream of invective, which, in the art that is blasphemy and profanity, was the greatest work of its time.

Quite unfortunately, sitting about six feet away in the bleachers, looking both stricken and deeply disappointed, was my God-fearing and ever-correct grandmother. Like everyone else that day, she hadn't seen the treachery. She later quietly mentioned that how one handles defeat defines one much more so than how one handles victory. I told her that losing defined you as a loser. Further disappointment.

Playing pickup basketball with my children has been a great joy to me, a couple of girls and an old guy beating up on some moussed up high school boys who have no concept of a pass much less a pick and roll. Defense? Are they on iTunes? However, the girls have asked me never to indicate that I know them or am related to them in any way during a game.

I recently took care of a patient who couldn't seem to remember her medicines or her medical history or really much of anything. She confessed that her husband "always sort of took care of those things—he just enjoyed caring for me." He had recently been swept away by a vicious malignancy, gone a few months after diagnosis. After over 45 years of marriage.

Suddenly her world is full of empty spaces. Having lovingly leaned on someone for so long, her balance is gone. The other side of the bed looms as a grave. The quiet is leaden and liquid.

Three months ago my mother, just short of 88 years, fun and clear and chipper (albeit porcelain frail), rejoined my father, probably on the shores of Lindbergh Lake in the Swan Valley.

When I have written my columns, I have emailed them to my wife Pam and then to Mom, to screen for blatantly offensive content. Like my grandmother, they have come to accept the moderately offensive. It is weird now not to hear her commentary and diplomatic rejoinders.

I walk in the evenings, and part of that ritual had been a phone call to Mom. We would talk sports, politics, kids, work, everything. I know she prepped for those conversations. She told me that growing older meant you had to work at being relevant and informed. "No one cares about how you used to do it or what is was like in my day." I lift the phone to dial, and, well, I can't anymore.

I know that to lose her meant she never had dementia, never had the humiliation of incontinence, and died with plans and promise. A woman of great faith, she lives, I know. I am sorry for my loss most of all. A bad loser rarely reforms.

Grief is a real illness, I think frequently underestimated. Although sad, my mother's death was the finale to a great symphony. I can't imagine losing a child or spouse. Many are forced to.

There are no pills or treatments for grief. What works very well is interest and attention. I think we are afraid of grieving people sometimes, feeling awkward. The solution to the problem of finding words is to not find them. Just show up.

I will honor her by being more fun as I age, not less. I won't whine about my illnesses or complain about how indolent kids are these days. She told me to practice being old when you are young so you would have the hang of it.

Will I become a better loser? Nah.

Do you want a surgeon who is a good loser?

Soggy Filters

You never know when it might be you. Or your kid.

A lot of people, from techs to nurses to surgeons to coordinators to administrators, work very hard to make sure the trauma systems in the area are excellent.

They drill and refine and study so that when the time comes when everything has to go not only perfectly, but RIGHT NOW, the "Golden Hour" of trauma is a life-saving ballet of efficiency.

Because someday, the most precious person in their lives might hang on the precipice between life and death.

The refinement of a trauma system involves the care of a great deal of drunks.

Drunk people tend to hang out with other drunk people. Drunk people tend, as you may have heard, to say ill-advised things to other drunk people, or to hit on their girlfriends.

Since the offended party is also drunk, their filter for reaction is a little soggy, so they might punch, shoot, or stab the ill-mannered Drunk #1. This creates a "Trauma Activation."

It is not uncommon that, upon encountering the injured party, a health care provider will also wish to punch, shoot, or stab the "victim"—

often in a short period of time. Being hauled in an ambulance to the Emergency Department, perhaps bleeding to death, does not seem to improve the social skills of the average drunk.

Such was the case when a gentleman presented with a stab wound to the abdomen. The trauma surgeon was unable, after careful exploration of the wound in the ER, to determine if the knife had entered the inside of the abdomen and injured any organs. Surgical exploration was required.

Mike Hovland was the anesthesiologist, who, at just after 2:00 A.M., interviewed the bellicose and inebriated "victim" just prior to surgery. Mike noted that the patient complained of difficult "asthma," and coincidentally smoked two packs a day.

Mike suggested that there might be a causal connection between the two, and that smoking cessation might dramatically improve the asthma.

To which the patient responded, "**** you."

Mike, who is about the kindest and least judgmental person to ever don scrubs, was taken aback.

The trauma surgeon, who was close by, and none too pleased to be there at such an hour on a weekday, heard the exchange and told the patient, somewhat less kindly, that antagonizing the person who was about to take your life in their hands was a very bad idea. Good point.

Especially when you are getting all this care for free. The chance of a shot or stabbed drunk having health insurance at 2:00 in the morning is 0.001%. I didn't actually look that up, but it probably isn't that high.

I would likely have taken the opportunity to put on a glove, stick a finger in that wound, and try one more time to see if it really did go into the belly. It is probably a wonder I still have a license. Thank God for those filters.

Mike, on the other hand, was taken aback by the response. He felt he had provoked a negative exchange, and later told his father Jim Hovland, a retired physician.

"Michael," he intoned in a way only dads can intone, "I, as a general rule, avoid giving life advice to drunks at 2:00 A.M.—in particular, drunks who have been recently stabbed."

I am often amazed at the professionalism among all the trauma care providers, despite being hit, kicked, spit upon, and barfed upon. Did I mention the smell? Yet they do their jobs as if they were caring for some dear church lady.

This includes law enforcement. I would have shot, tasered, or clubbed most of these characters before they ever got to the ER. A cop brought a guy in one time with a busted-up face, picked up off the street, drunk and fighting. The cop very politely asked me if he might possibly have a warm blanket, because he thought the poor guy might be cold.

It is at 2:00 A.M., when we are tired and churlish, when we are spit upon and trash talked, that we truly discern the meaning of a life of service. "As you do to the least of me, you do to me."

So, reflecting upon all this, let me give you this advice:

Nah, forget it.

You might have been drinking.

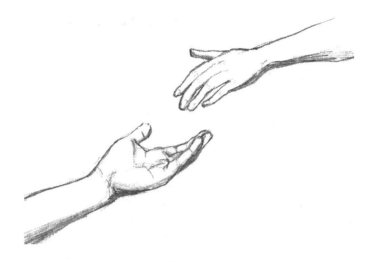

4） COOL PEOPLE

Nothing elucidates the true character of an individual like the application of the life blowtorches known as stress, pressure, and adversity. A gentleman surgeon becomes a gibbering maniac when bleeding becomes brisk. A snarky sophisticate becomes a pale puddle when given a threatening diagnosis. Because all of our airs and pretentions and degrees and titles are necessarily toted about by a fallible corpus of guts and bone, illness quickly teaches us that life is much more of a street fight than a salon.

Yet what forces us to confront the grubby also conspires to reveal greatness. Extreme circumstance will yield the most transcendent and selfless human behavior. These next stories are of remarkable individuals who privately and quietly display the best of human nature in the most difficult of situations.

Neighbors

Annie was, she thought, somewhere around 80. When I saw her in the wound clinic, she was suffering from moderate dementia as well as the large venous ulcer on her leg. Accompanying her was Mike, a young man in his late 20s.

Both were pretty disheveled, and both were redolent of unwashed bodies and rarely changed clothes. The macerated wound on her leg added to the bouquet.

I asked the young man what his relationship to Annie was. "Neighbor," he answered. Apparently he had been doing the dressing changes for her and accompanied her, on the bus, to the clinic appointments.

He had moved into the unit next to Annie, in a low-income apartment building, without ever having known her. He saw that she was alone and confused at times. A bit of a lost soul himself, he started helping her out.

Mike looked not at all comfortable in the situation, but asked good questions and listened intently to the wound-care directions. I was relieved that he did not inquire about pain medications. He agreed to take her to a public primary care clinic to work on her blood sugars.

I told him I thought what he was doing was pretty cool. He frowned and squirmed and said, "There wasn't no choice."

Yeah, Mike, there was a choice. Neighbors can drive by each other in their luxury SUVs for years and never know each other's names. Kids are hauled in those same vehicles for miles to play with other kids, but never play with the kid down the street.

To be a neighbor or not is not a matter of physical proximity. It is a matter of choice.

In Mike's mind, caring for another in need was what a decent neighbor did. There wasn't no choice for Mike.

Societies are composed of units, the first of which is the family. The next essential building block is a cluster of families, and that is a neighborhood.

Cohesive neighborhoods make a better society, and cohesive neighborhoods are a choice we make, not a coincidence or a matter of fate. It is a choice that involves effort, an effort that might involve a trip outside our comfort zone.

"Well, Mike," I said, "you've done a good job."

"Aw," he mumbled, "anybody'd do it."

Would we?

A Bit of a List

My patient was an attractive, well put-together woman of 72.

"My neck is simply ridiculous. I don't mind aging, but I have a size-sixteen neck on a size-six frame. I make turkeys look svelte."

I reviewed the procedure to correct excess neck skin, which she patiently endured, having read and viewed every available resource on the Web. She likely knew my seventh-grade math grades.

"Are you otherwise healthy?" I inquired. "We will need some sort of anesthetic."

"Oh, yes," she replied. "I walk every day and work 30 hours a week at a non-profit. I will be fine with this."

"Good," I continued. "Any operations?"

"Well, there were those two heart valves, which are fine now, and quite a small brain tumor. It was benign."

Heart valves? Brain Tumor?

"My heart function is excellent and the valves competent. No reason not to operate on some redundant neck skin."

"Okay," I ventured on, "how about medications?"

"Well, there is of course the Coumadin."

Coumadin? You mean the blood thinner kind?

"Yes, well, you simply stop it five days before the neck lift and it shouldn't be an issue. They did that with my back surgery."

"You didn't mention the back surgery."

"Long time ago and hardly relevant now."

"How about other medications?" I could hardly wait.

"Well, with the rheumatoid arthritis, the Enbrel and the prednisone keep my hands working." Now I noticed her hands.

"I suppose you will fuss about healing with those drugs, but I can endure being off a month, which is what they did when I had the partial colectomy."

Of course, the partial colectomy. Only partial.

She gave me a hard look. "I realize that there is a bit of a list there. However, I always do well, I don't have complications, and I don't complain. You've done much larger operations on much older, sicker people. I also need to get back to work."

Gnarled hands, heart valves, brain tumors, and rat poison medications.

Oh, and perfectly well, thank you, please quit dawdling and fix my neck.

With this "bit of a list" she could easily hang out a sign saying, "I am old and sick." Instead, she wants to look good while she tries to help people who don't always smell good.

She accepts no definition of herself as old or sick. Many do, however, and any physician can tell you how many young people are on disability for various, ill-defined maladies.

We define ourselves as cheerful or gloomy. Positive or whiny. Team-builder or gossip. We define ourselves as an ill person, or as a vibrant person with this "bit of a list."

My father, a WWII guy, defined men either as those who fought with their brothers in combat or those who ran. Even after the war, he knew who was who.

Often in our lives we feel misunderstood. People don't "get" us. But are we projecting what we really are? If I am not warm and approachable to my patients and my staff, should I be surprised if they are wary? If I wallow about in my medical issues, will anyone want me at their Super Bowl party?

On her way out, she said she had one more question.

"When can I go back to the gym?"

Confidence

Seattle Seahawks running back Marshawn Lynch has battered opposing defenders both with his formidable "beastieness" and the unwavering confidence that those seeking to stop him had better update their disability policies. Three, four guys can't stop him. The only thing that can stop him is a microphone. He has no confidence when it comes to public speaking.

I love to speak to large crowds, and I have no compunction at all about taking apart a chest or a belly. But I can't drive the Beartooth Highway, because heights turn me into a wimpsicle.

Think about the crazy chemical that is confidence. A guy leads a major golf tournament for 71 holes, then drops three in a row in the water. A kicker for the Vikings was 35/35 during the season, and missed a 31-yarder to send them to the Super Bowl.

For better or worse, surgeons know a lot about confidence. Things go well, and you think you are a pretty bad dude; but an unexpected death or a disastrous complication, and you're not sure you can tie your shoes without losing three units of blood.

Many of my cancer patients struggle with their confidence. After surgery, chemo, and a dessert of radiation, they're not sure they can grocery shop, much less go back to work. Older patients come to feel that traveling in a busy airport or even going to church is more daunting than rewarding.

Physical confidence is especially fascinating. On a daily basis I render opinions about eyes, noses, ears, jowls, necks, breasts, tummies, thighs, tushes, love handles, saddle bags, banana rolls, wrinkles, rumples, lumps, bumps, and wattles. The motivations for these evaluations are all over the map. "My grandchild pulled on my wattle." (I love grandchildren–they will add 10 feet to my boat.) "I can't look old in my business." "I am divorced and on the market." "Wedding pictures are in six months." "I look like a basset hound."

I would say that two times in three, I'm pretty much in agreement with the patient. This isn't Beverly Hills—our patients are pretty sensible. If you are a fit 35-year-old mom with a grand total of two ounces of breast tissue, and those two ounces happen to be residing somewhere around your waist, I see your point. Fixing a specific problem is gratifying for the surgeon and for the patient.

But once in three, maybe, I sense a more complex lack of physical, often sexual, confidence. A patient will tell me "I can't look at myself, much less let my partner see me." On exam, I see a not perfect but perfectly normal and appealing body. I try to communicate, in a non-creepy way (not easy, by the way), that their body is fine the way it is. Let's try to fix your confidence.

I doubt there is anyone who is completely physically confident.
I've never been good looking, so imagine what being nearly 57 and bald has done to improve that. You have your own list of issues, I'm sure. So how do we deal with the issue of physical confidence?

Start with the "Lord grant me the serenity to accept what I cannot change" thing. OK, I can't change my age, and I'm not going to wear a rug or spend 300,000 clams on hair transplants (that was the low bidder). But I can keep the weight off and maintain a little muscle tone. I can spend less time in scrubs (glorified pajamas). I can smile more and whine less, both of which make a person more attractive. I can notice people more. My late father always shined his shoes.

Lack of confidence often derives from the perception that we don't have control, and thinking we don't have control is often an excuse.

You think you can't lose weight because your knees are bad? Try the swimming pool. You think you can't lose weight because you have a (metabolic syndrome, low thyroid, hormone imbalance, fill in the blank)?" Show me one guy on a raft on the Pacific for 50 days who didn't lose half his body weight. The laws of physics haven't been revoked. You burn more, take in less, and you lose. To improve your physical confidence, make a list of everything you can control, and attack it. The rest you let go. Make sure it is an honest list.

I am fearful we have become a society of disabilities, of syndromes, of disorders, of diseases, of diagnoses. All of us are a few fries short of a Happy Meal, and certainly some are legitimately disadvantaged. But a culture of excuses rarely yields greatness.

The most effective way to acquire confidence, physical or otherwise, is to get outside of yourself. If I see a guy with a metal fencepost poking in his cheek and out his forehead, all of a sudden, it is not about me.

If you don't love yourself, go love somebody else and see what happens.

The first time I brought my future wife to Montana, I had known her for just a couple of months. My parents' home in Polson, MT, had been hit with a big storm right before we came, so the visit consisted of cleaning up a huge mess and making repeated trips to the Polson dump. As I watched her unload truckload after truckload into that soggy and fetid mess, I thought, "This person might have potential."

There are lots of ways to be sexy.

Tatoo

Women of a certain age can tell you that men of a certain age become, well, goofy. Forget the boringly cliché extramarital affairs and drug issues; the average sixth-decade male is more likely to develop a crush on something both motorized and financially disastrous. This summer I had an infatuation with a side-by-side ATV, sort of like a Jeep with no roof, doors, floor, or bumpers. And it costs a lot more. I don't know if it is hormones or a looming sense of mortality, but male mentalpause is expensive.

My latest ambition is to become a true artist in the tattoo realm. The last step in breast reconstruction is the creation of a realistic looking nipple and areola. I have become a disciple of Vinnie, sort of a creepy/scary looking dude, similar to the meth-cooking punk on *Breaking Bad*. A tattoo guy from Maryland, he is the guru of the 3-D nipple/areolar tattoo. Rather immodestly, and in no small part due to Vinnie's YouTube videos, I think I am approaching "Vinnie status."

The other day I finished up a double breast reconstruction, doing my best 3-D tattoo on a very patient woman who tolerated my buzzing and fussing.

I then belatedly ran across the hall to see another patient young woman who had just received the diagnosis of breast cancer. She had had a fair bit of education regarding breast reconstruction (she had chosen mastectomy), but didn't feel like she really had a grasp of what it was all about. She had an intellectual, but not visceral, understanding of the process.

I scooted across the hall just as my recently tattooed patient was getting to leave. I nervously asked her if she wouldn't mind showing our new patient her completed result. She graciously agreed. The few minutes we spent demonstrating the anatomy and technique of the reconstruction was worth more than a thousand words. Our new patient came away with the belief that it could be done, and she could do it.

I was struck by the generosity of so many breast cancer patients who are willing to share the most intimate of their experiences.

I was struck by the delicate lightning that is female connection, especially when the emotional stakes are high.

I was struck that some of the most breathtakingly elegant moments in our lives are unexpected; small but perfect diamonds of empathic brilliance.

I was struck by the realization that I am very privileged to do what I do.

The one thing I have learned from the remarkable women in my life is that relationships rather than pistons determine the extent of our riches.

Alas, a surgeon cannot change his spots.

Do I pass on the ATV to save up for the boat? I'll ask Vinnie.

Dog with a Bone

The nice lady from the Billings Clinic medical records department was polite but firm—she would really appreciate my dictating a delinquent operative report from about a month ago. Perhaps I hadn't seen the 64 written requests she had sent me? The patient had had a very protracted hospitalization, and payment could not be received until the record was complete. Certainly she didn't wish to chain me to the back of a pickup truck and drag me down a gravel road after having extracted my fingernails, but....

Talk about a thankless job—getting hundreds of providers to do their homework is like trying to get as many perfect math papers out of recalcitrant fifth-graders.

So I looked up the patient's record on the computer, seeking absolution. The guy presented with a diagnosis of esophageal cancer that was pretty advanced, having grown into the chest wall. Dr. John Gregory had removed the esophagus and made a tube out of the stomach and had pulled it up into the chest to make sort of a new esophagus. All that surgery and the damage by the tumor had created a pretty big hole on the front of the chest, and my part had been to bring a flap of muscle and skin from the back to fill it in.

I really enjoy those kinds of big, complex cases. They are a combination of problem solving and construction. Working with other surgical colleagues is fun, too, like playing pickup hoops.

When I went to dictate the case, though, I was astonished how extensive the record was. I counted something like 15 different trips to the operating room.

With complex wounds and the debility brought on by esophageal cancer (can't eat, lose weight, malnourished), the only way a patient can survive is if the wound is kept meticulously clean, which means going back to the OR for debridement (cleaning and trimming) over and over again. It takes a lot of time, and Medicare pays enough for that procedure that you could afford a six-pack of Old Milwaukee. Not Miller Lite.

Dr. Gregory stayed with that guy, day after day, procedure after procedure, week after week. Just kept whittling, cleaning, tweaking the meds and nutrition, and generally being a dog with a bone.

John is a quiet, taciturn guy. He will not be invited to be a game-show host. He substitutes schmoozing and glad-handing with dogged determination.

One of the ennobling aspects of our humanity is the extraordinary diversity in the ways in which we express our concern for others.

Whenever I visited home during my years in training, my father would always wash the windshield and check the tires and oil of my car. Sometimes new tires would appear without comment.

How many people in your life have shown their love by feeding you? Thousands of loads of laundry have their own eloquence. A friend drags you out of a fight. A teacher flogs you until you can write a coherent sentence. A coach turns a wimp into a force. And a surgeon scrapes away a little bit of pus every other day for weeks.

Love with action, wordless love, to me speaks most significantly. I've always told my wife that guys big into flowers and date nights probably have something on the side. She does not believe this.

Every job has its grind, its routine, and its records. What separates a job from a life ministry is not the content, whether it is peeling logs or saving lives, but the portion of our soul and the extent of the effort that we bring to the charge.

My records are done, for now, and my fingernails intact. Tomorrow I will start it all over again. It is good to have a place to be, a job to do, and people to care for.

5) CHARACTERS

The most interesting characters I have encountered in medicine are no doubt similar to the most interesting people you know: They are vexingly complex, impossible to categorize, and ceaselessly entertaining. They can be unreliable, treacherous, and lovable at the same time. Many of them are as brilliant as they are deeply flawed. Con artists, alcoholics, and geniuses often occupy the same parking slots, whether it is medicine, art, or athletics.

King Lear

I spent the summer of 2004 in Jackson, Mississippi, beginning the second and final year of my plastic surgery residency. My family had retreated to Montana, escaping the molten heat and honey-like humidity of the Southern summer.

This Friday night was a "hand call" night, meaning every gang gunshot wound involving a hand, every firework-blown finger, and every turkey slicer-sliced thumb would be mine. Action was inevitable, sleep unlikely.

My faculty backup that night was Dr. Richard Lear, our department chairman, and a pretty facile hand guy. Since his wife was away, and my family far north, he suggested we spend the evening at his country home, dining and awaiting the inevitable mayhem.

We rode through the dense, dark woods, the narrow two-lane black ribbon beneath us consumed by his Mercedes at a rather alarming rate.

The 1840s-era white home on his sprawling property had seen Confederate armies and domestic slaves. The night was alive with both the light and the noise of innumerable insects, and the grass rustled with the motion of critters unknown.

We sat on the capacious porch, the ghosts politely quiet around us, and relished the barbeque we had acquired at a shack along the way.

Dr. Lear produced a fine Southern bourbon, which I declined because I was on call. He expressed disappointment, in that he saw drinking as a form of collegial communion. He also felt that no competent, experienced surgeon would be unable to perform his duties due simply to a little bourbon.

He had long, white hair and a white beard, and looked as if he could step back in time and lead a Confederate regiment. An erudite man, he had the same command of literature and music as he did of hand surgery. He wrote and recorded very credible folk-guitar albums. Our porch conversations ranged from arts to politics to history, and the bourbon evaporated with the passage of the hours.

We sparred gently in the Faulknerian night, he an unrepentant, well traveled socialist, and I a homebody father of three. The angry yap of the call beeper impaled our amiable reverie.

Sure enough, some guy had cut his thumb clean off with a skill saw, and our services were required to replant the digit. Thumbs are important.

The once full bourbon bottle was empty, and Dr. Lear scooped up his keys and suggested we get going. I offered to drive, and he just appeared amused.

We were about three miles down the asphalt path when we saw flashing lights ahead. The highway patrol had set up roadblocks to identify drunk drivers. Well, I thought, this will be interesting—do I bail him out first or fix the thumb?

Dr. Lear then flawlessly chatted up the patrolman—he knew him, of course—and passed through without a puff on the Breathalyzer.

In the operating room we dissected out the arteries and veins in the nicely chilled and detached thumb, then found the corresponding vessels in the hand. Out came the microscope, and we began connecting things.

I began by sewing the thumb artery back to its mate on the hand. Dr. Lear started to fidget after a few stitches, and although I thought I did a pretty good job, it was clearly too slow for him. He then proceeded to sew the other artery and the two veins flawlessly in half the time I did it. All after a fifth of bourbon. No tremor, never an extra motion.

We finished up at 6 A.M., and Dr. Lear got ready to head off to a recording session with his guitar. I couldn't keep my eyes open.
We had our struggles in my two years there—his affluent liberalism versus my judgmental conservatism, his alcoholism clashing with my sense of professional piety.

So often we have improbable affection for those so different from ourselves. Maybe they are mirror images of ourselves, so similar yet fundamentally inverted. Those relationships are best not judged or intellectually evaluated but rather just enjoyed, like fireflies in the Southern night.

Isaac the Great

Isaac would just appear, spectrally, as if he had some intracranial receiver for the frequency of my distress. I was struggling with some gangbanger who'd been shot in the arm. "Hand call" at the University of Mississippi in Jackson was a succession of these types of cases, as well as shredded hands from the turkey processing plant.

A guy was thrashing and screaming at me, two hundred mikes of fentanyl being an insult to the guy, me trying to torture him because I'm a racist (***), his boys going to take me down, etc.

Issac rolled into the ER cubicle (you wouldn't call it a room, mostly a sheet between beds) and began putting on a blue plastic glove. Like a great actor, he didn't overdo it, but rather effectively communicated his intent, which to both my erstwhile drug entrepreneur and me appeared to have unpleasant undertones.

To say Isaac's look at the guy was malevolent or baleful or withering would be a pale understatement. The room seemed to get colder, the lights somehow dimmer. His obsidian stubble in contrast to hospital-flourescent pale skin intensified the menace. The recently rambunctious patient looked scared. I was scared.

"While I am examining this injury," Isaac intoned in his Ukrainian-immigrant/Jewish/via-Brooklyn accent, softly, like he was speaking a mass, "I will explain your standing here."

"This is the only trauma hospital in the state of Mississippi—the others having been sued out of the gun-fighting business. In addition, you certainly don't have health insurance or any assets you are willing to share with us."

Isaac then inserted his index finger into the wound on the forearm, probing for the ends of the shattered radius, manually speculating about the status of the median nerve.

The patient wailed loudly, sweat popping all over his body, his eyes fluttering as his vagus nerve pulled the plug on his blood pressure. No one in the ER even looked up.

"So you see," Isaac continued, "we are the only persons on the planet who can help you. Yet you behave badly." I either heard or felt a crunching sensation. My blood pressure was getting a little low, too. "So if we are to restore function to your currently useless limb, you will need to be cooperative and respectful. Oh, and don't give me any of that racial crap. I got more check boxes than you have jewelry."

Isaac explained his tactics to me later, as we were scrubbing our hands in preparation for the repairs in the operating room. "You've got to understand the dynamic here," he said. "It's just like where I grew up in Brooklyn. These guys understand power and dominance, and once you set that straight, things are OK." He then proceeded to do a perfect repair of the bones, nerves, and tendons in that arm, as if the guy were some VIP. "The guy means nothing to me; even less, it appears, to himself. But my work, that's my thing, and it's gotta be OK for me."

Isaac had failed his general surgery boards just before I joined the plastic surgery residency, and was extremely upset and frustrated. I coached him and generally reformatted his approach to the oral exams, and he passed. Grateful, he became my protector.

He also thought it was cool that I had been a heart surgeon. He had been headed that way until a disagreement with a faculty member in his general surgery program resulted in said faulty member ending up in a dumpster, alive but indignant.

When I had repeated conflicts with a particular faculty member, Isaac offered to have a Russian associate from Brooklyn come down and take care of the guy. "Only 10,000 bucks, airfare included." Isaac, of course, would pay for it by moonlighting a couple of weekends at some little town deep in the Mississippi woodlands. "There are way too many of these old KGB guys sitting around up there around New York. They need something to do."

He always had the most amazing presentations for our conferences, having figured out how to download PowerPoint presentations from the Internet before anyone knew you could do that. He had the answers to the written board exams before the exams. He had Grand Theft Auto updates hacked from European websites before they were published in this country. My 10-year-old son regarded him as something of a shaman.

Isaac expected people to act in their own self-interest, to grab whatever they could get, and to exploit situations when possible. Since he expected so little, he wasn't disappointed, and wasted no effort in judgment. He only played the cards he could see.

Yet he was remarkably kind—not because he expected any return or had any sort of agenda, but because he chose to be kind. It made him feel good. He was, and is, a deeply moral guy, but in a customized way.

I miss my protector, someone who can stare down scary dudes or put out a hit on an annoying personality. I suppose I should be able to take care of myself by now. But one of life's richest experiences is to protect, and be protected; to care, and be cared for, whether you need it or not.

Perhaps having someone whacked, as a gesture of concern, is a bit much. But it is the thought that counts.

Valedictorian or Quarterback?

I trained in cardiac surgery in the 1980s. Since the field was basically invented in the 1950s, at some point or another I got to meet just about every founding father and warlord who created and shaped the discipline. It was like having a beer with Thomas Jefferson and George Washington.

Back in the good old days, when it was legal, Medtronic, a heart valve company, would fly graduating heart surgeon trainees to a conference. They attracted us by paying all expenses, feeding and boozing us lavishly, and putting on a program with talks by some of the biggest names in the field. Some of the older speakers, having missed the big-money years of the field, probably appreciated the paycheck.

One of these Greats, purring from Scotch, was bemused when I commented that it must have been cool to have been present at the Creation.

"You guys. See, you have to understand how it was. We were scientists trying to solve a problem. We were trying to operate on something that you can't operate on if it is moving—you know, the heart. But if it isn't moving, then, well, you're dead."

(Sip). "The first heart surgeries were on kids, of course—they would die terribly of these congenital problems, and so our efforts were there primarily. Hell, we tried freezing them in tubs of ice, then quick cutting them open while they were essentially preserved by the cold. We hooked children up to their mothers, so the mother's heart would support the child's circulation while we worked."

(More of a slurp). "At some point we hit on the idea of using a pump to circulate the blood, running it through this device to bubble oxygen into the blood as well. Big, crude machines. But it started to work."

"But you guys. See, we were scientists, scientists who operated. You guys are more like professional athletes, slick hands, fast, like racehorses bred for a task. None of us probably would make the team now."

(A frank slug). "We had to invent clamps that didn't cut arteries in half, needles that didn't shred, and oxygenators that wouldn't turn the blood into cocktail mix. You guys cry like babies if the drapes are the wrong color."

(Moist eyes). "You guys. You go into therapy if you lose a couple of patients a year. We were lucky to save one in three. We lost so many kids. No, it wasn't cool. But it had to be done, and we did what we could do."

I've pondered those comments over the years. The Surgical Scientist vs. the Surgical Athlete. It is a tale of two cultures.

The chief of my cardiac surgery program, Don Grey, had made his reputation as a scientist, building on the work of his mentor involving abnormal heart rhythms. They used a surgical approach to problems that had defied medical treatment, and created a great deal of interest in a field that, after 40 years of rapid evolution, had begun to stagnate a bit.

Rising rapidly through the ranks of academia, he published amazing surgical results. Everything was 100% successful, it seemed, which mystified us trainees taking care of the same procedures' carnage. He traveled the world as a great man and surgeon, and no one was concerned that they had difficulty replicating such magic.

If the emperor had no clothes, we weren't going to say anything—we just wanted to get our ticket punched and to get out of there. We dreaded working with him, because since he was a Great Surgeon who spent all his time lecturing and traveling, he had a hard time finding a rhythm operating when he was home.

Wardell, on the other hand, we revered. He hardly ever spoke. In fact, he finally had to hire a lovely woman to speak to families and patients. He had the soulless demeanor of a great white shark. He wore those wooden clog shoes, which accentuated his already towering presence. We had to use a couple of stools to stand with him at the operating table. Rather than berate you, he would stomp the wooden shoe on the floor in irritation. It was like having your spine slapped.

The best you could do was to stay out of his way. I often suspected that he had no cerebral cortex, that his hands connected directly to his cerebellum. His movements were so effortlessly darting and efficient that my own cortex felt like dispirited yogurt. I dreaded the wooden stomp.

He could do things no one else could do. Cases that mere mortals couldn't do because of the length of time the heart would have to be stopped were routine for him. One week he did 17 open heart cases and was chafing Friday afternoon that he had all this time left, and all the cardiologists were probably already at their lake homes, the lazy parasites, instead of generating more cases for him to do.

His relationship with Grey was tense at best. Wardell probably generated four million a year in fees, at least, and Grey, as chairman, paid him probably $500,000. Grey, of course, took more.

Wardell did little clinical research, but did publish impressive clinical series, albeit infrequently. He saw no point in generating paper for paper's sake. His contempt for paper-tiger academicians like Grey was extremely well disguised, and therefore more potent. Grey knew intuitively that the valedictorian would never match the quarterback of the football team on the Man Scale, and the obvious reverence we trainees had for Wardell infuriated Grey.

Because he was so high-profile, Grey ended up operating on the politicians and society-types. Wardell did the businessmen, mobsters, and, most importantly, the doctors who needed heart surgery. This was not lost on Grey. When one of the residents had Wardell do his mother's surgery, I thought Grey would fire him.

The Surgical Scientist develops concepts and procedures based on his understanding of human biology and anatomy. He is convinced, almost religiously at times, that a certain idea must be right. It can result in game-changing miracles, or in hubristic carnage. The Scientist is revered world-wide, and often sniggered at in his own institution.

The Surgical Athlete, as it were, bases his techniques on what works, not what should work. He sifts through all the smoke from the Scientists, and does what makes sense to him. He relies heavily on other cool guys like himself. They find each other quickly. He has the admiration of the nurses, residents, and the more astute referring physicians. He may not be a great innovator, but he will get you home alive.

The poor consumer/patient, of course, has no idea about any of this. The most exalted institution, the most hyped surgeon, can be perfectly deadly for the unwitting layman. If you see "Five Star Rating" or "Top Hospital in the State," maybe you should consider "Run for Your Life."

I wonder about the future of the great Surgical Athlete, those with skill and ambition and a rapacious appetite for more cases. When I applied for a cardiac surgery residency, there were hundreds of applicants for 80 spots. Now there are 70 applicants for 120 positions.

The surgeons of the late 70s, 80s, and early 90s clear-cut vast forests of green. They charged Medicare and the insurance companies whatever number came into their heads. They operated on anyone who wasn't bolted to the floor. The cardiac guys, especially, made millions. The talent flocked to the money.

I understand that there are priests and teachers and such who genuinely don't care about money, but not, for the most part, the Surgical Athlete. If they are going to endure a long, punishing training period, rack up huge debt, and be subjected to grinding anxiety and death and lawsuits, they want to be paid, and paid well.

In the future, you will likely be operated upon by a kind, gentle soul who may have served a mission in Guatemala, which impressed the medical school admissions committee. He/she will have served a very humane residency with reasonable working hours. He/she will not be motivated by greed or promise of riches (as there won't be any), but rather by a desire to serve and apply sound scientific principles. The carnivorous entrepreneurs with the All-Pro hands will be starting something up in Silicon Valley.

I have decided, at this rather late point in my career, that I am content with being Very Good, rather than Great. Whether one is a great Surgical Scientist or Surgical Athlete, or a great something else, there is an extreme character, a certain too-muchness in the Great that I might find appealing or appalling but would rather not see in myself.

Will someday some company pay me to tell stories? Probably not, but I will still tell stories. I can buy my own beer.

6) SALLY'S STORY

"Sally's Story" is an account of my daughter Sally's encounter with a brain tumor called "acoustic neuroma." The original idea was to demonstrate how a highly trained and extremely savvy doctor, not to mention devoted and protective father, approached a complex medical decision and did the right thing for his baby.

It didn't turn out that way.

Despite all the research, the pestering of experts, the deliberate decision process, and complete wiring of all contingencies, her surgery resulted in the most dreaded of complications. Her face was paralyzed, and she lost the hearing in her right ear.

What was a 1% risk preoperatively was a 100% reality postoperatively, and our journey through this process and this disappointment is the basis of these several stories. I did not want to keep writing about what had turned into a disaster, but Sally insisted that we needed to follow the story through. Her courage and perseverance through a devastating injury, the support our family received, and her early and promising recovery created a remarkable storyline we couldn't have anticipated. These articles follow that storyline as it happened.

For the hundreds of you who rooted for her and prayed for her and directly contributed to her recovery, we thank you again.

The Diagnosis—The Other Side

For years I coached kids' basketball and probably annoyed a few referees with my querulous jawing. Then I had to referee, and all of a sudden things were faster and more confused than I realized on the other side.

Late in the summer my oldest daughter, Sally, a NICU nurse at the University of Washington in Seattle, developed a sense of fullness and pain in her right ear, as well as intermittent facial numbness. She was treated without success for an ear infection, and after pestering the ENT clinic (more jawing), she finally had an MRI. I expected some sort of an infection or swelling.

But not a tumor. An acoustic neuroma is a rare tumor (1 in 100,000) that is inside the skull and involves the nerve of hearing and balance. It is not cancerous, but it grows and eventually destroys hearing and presses on the brainstem. The tumor is right next to the nerve that moves facial muscles and can paralyze those, leaving the face looking like a bad stroke.

All of a sudden we were on the other side, learning a whole lot about acoustic neuromas, also called vestibular schwannomas. You can do three things. The tumor can be observed, but we decided against that as she is only 25, she was already symptomatic, and her tumor is smaller, so the outcomes are better with treatment. There is a treatment called "gamma knife," which is highly focused radiation. It does not kill or remove the tumor, but keeps it from growing. The other option is to do a craniotomy (pop your noggin) and remove it.

We combed the scientific literature on the subject and identified the world authorities. We spoke to the gamma-knife guru at NYU, a highly published guy at UCLA, and several big hitters in Seattle.

The radiation guys said, "No question, gamma knife is the way to go. That argument is over." The surgeons said, "Get the thing out—do you really want to cook your brain?"

I've never encountered anything in medicine where the opinions are so polar, the arguments so emphatic, and the picture for the patient is so unclear.

Frankly, most of my surgical decisions take about 30 seconds. The right thing to do is almost always pretty obvious. In fact, most patients know what they need before they see a surgeon. The hardest part for Sally, I think, was wrestling with the statistics, weighing the risks of radiation versus a facial nerve injury, and dealing with the idea of a tumor in her head. Uncertainty seems at times to be worse than most certainties.

She has decided on the surgery. The long-term risks of radiation are concerning, and if the radiation doesn't work, the surgery is much harder. Her tumor is currently favorable for surgery. She is symptomatic and wants relief, although that too is uncertain.

We made our own decision, because it seemed everyone had a hammer, and all the world was a nail.

We sought out The Man, a high-volume operator with lots of experience in a rare tumor. Who happened to live in Seattle. Who happened to be a medical school classmate of mine. Who I happened to have played with on a med school intramural basketball team.

Johnny D is a very confident, charismatic neurosurgeon who told us he had done 900 of these, and in his hands her risk of facial nerve injury was 3%. He thought here was a 60% chance she would keep her hearing. The time to do it, he said, is now, while it is favorable.

We were soothed by his presentation, but I also remembered that Johnny D never saw a shot in those basketball games he wouldn't take. He probably thinks he was an 80% shooter. An old friend of mine, an anesthesiologist who works with him and also played on that team, said, "He's very good, but he is still a gunner." We don't escape our past.

I feel like we are at peace with our decision—I just wish we could change places. I would rather have my head cracked than sit in that waiting room. This is tougher on Mom, because while I understand Sally's anxiety, Mom feels every bit of it. Moms can't help it—that's what they do.

I will go to Seattle in a few days. I will stay a week, and my wife maybe two or three (which ought to be interesting). Sally has been remarkably cool, and I will try to follow her lead. No wonder surgery waiting rooms smell like a brewery.

And I'll keep my mouth shut. Whether it is a referee or a surgeon, you have to let people do their jobs.

In the Waiting Room

I am sitting in the surgical waiting area at Swedish Hospital in Seattle, trapped in a time warp. It is about four minutes since I last checked the time, and an impossibly vast chasm looms until Sally's operation will be completed. Rather than drift into gibbering madness, I will chat with you, Dear Reader, and perhaps you can distract me.

These columns for me are conversations—drinking inspirationally dark coffee in a cherished mug; sitting at a rustic wood-slab table near the fire; looking out the windows of a log home to a misting lake that is mirror-like in the early morning sun, perfectly reflecting the larch and ponderosa. Honey-wheat pancakes, ridden with huckleberries, rise to greatness on the griddle. Have a seat.

She was so composed and calm this morning, perhaps sensing that her mother and I would benefit more from a general anesthetic than she would. Sally is a neonatal ICU nurse, and manages the bereavement program for those who have lost their babies. I was being managed, and I appreciated it.

This hospital is another marvel of teak and maple, granite and marble, LED lighting and edgy art. I started my career as a nurse's aide in the early 70s at St. Patrick Hospital in Missoula—a brick edifice with those speckled stone floors, white walls, and multi-patient wards. I've worked in VA hospitals that resembled prisons. I sort of miss them.

Billings is certainly not lagging. The ICU at Billings Clinic looks like a Residence Inn, each room having a family area with a couch. I remember ICUs where one patient could easily reach over and suction the guy next to him. No flat-screen LED TVs, no polished maple.

The Orthopedic floor at St Vincent makes me want to break a hip so I can check in and chill for a while. It seems ironic to me that there is this frantic push to shorten hospital stays, to throw people out onto the streets with a skin stapler, saying, "Hey, would you mind closing the rest of your incision on the way home?" and then making the places so nice that no one in their right mind would ever want to leave.

I also wonder about the cost of all these designer sconces and Corian cafeteria tables. My omelet was excellent. Hospital food should be watery, (probably powdered) scrambled eggs scooped up in a metal spoon and contemptuously splattered on a chipped ceramic plate by a surly server who likely has done a little time.

As patients, we howl bitterly about stratospheric health care bills at the same time we wonder if the cafeteria will deliver a breve latte to our suite in the Cushy Care Unit. The hospital suits survey and drill down (business clichés abound in hospital executive suites), find out what we want, and give it to us.

We all say, "I don't want to be hooked up to a machine, just set me on the ol' iceberg and let me float away." Yet when the time comes, we submit ourselves and our family members to the most appalling and frequently futile interventions since the Spanish Inquisition. The great irony of a free and democratic, specifically capitalist, society is that we get what we ask for.

It is only 9:00. Wow. Four more hours. It is only in the extremity of my distress that I share this darkest thought—it is only a 30-minute walk down to the Ocean Alexander dealership on Lake Union, where there is a 68-foot yacht that is the epitome of all that is beautiful in life. I could be down and back in plenty of time. Do you think there is an actual devil? I never have. I think our own venality is more than sufficient.

In no universe am I glad this happened to my daughter. However, when this sort of train wrecks in your life, the only good comes from what you learn.

They did 3,000 craniotomies (brain surgeries) in this hospital last year. Crazy. But just one of them is our Mouse. I am going to be just a little more focused, a little more attentive, and a little more connected to each life and person and body I touch from now on.

I like the flat screens as much as the next guy. But health care lives at the personal level. When you are sick and frightened and there is darkness all around, and a light appears saying "I understand and I actually care," that is health care. Better yet, it is healing.

I think I will take a walk now. I don't like sitting on the bench. I'm the surgeon; other people sit on the bench and wait.

Not today. And no, I'm not going to the boat place.

A Twist in the Plot

The first bad sign was the length of the operation.

When I last wrote to you we were in the surgical waiting room at Swedish Hospital in Seattle, anxiously awaiting the conclusion of our daughter Sally's brain surgery. She had an acoustic neuroma, a tumor of the hearing and balance nerve, and after an exhaustive tour of every treatment option, she had chosen to have surgery.

Her tumor was small and favorably located in a bony canal at the base of the skull. The surgeons told her she had a 3% risk of injury, usually temporary, to the facial nerve, which controls all the movement on the right side of her face. She also had a 60% chance of keeping her hearing. Rather than wait for the tumor to get larger, or run the long-term risks of radiation, she opted to get it out of the way.

Finally, about two hours after we thought the procedure would be done, the two surgeons came to the waiting area. Grim-faced, they directed us to the private consultation area. Very bad sign.

We hadn't even sat down when the neurosurgeon blurted out, "We cut the facial nerve."

Often people describe the reception of really bad news as a sensation of being punched. I think it is more like an explosion that starts under your ribcage, with the fireball mushrooming into your chest and head, the world blurred and tilted.

Not only was the facial nerve gone, so was the hearing and balance nerve. So permanent deafness in the right ear, and a paralyzed right face. Everything we were trying to avoid.

In the ICU, as she awoke, she asked for my phone. Thoughtlessly, I gave it to her, and she did the "selfie" thing with the phone camera. "They bagged my facial nerve, didn't they?"

It is hard to describe the drop-down menu of this outcome. Because the balance nerve is gone, she has the spins and nausea all the time. The ear, even though deaf, roars like the ocean. She can't use a cup because her mouth won't hold in the liquid. Her right eye won't close, so she will have a weight inserted in the upper lid to make it close. Speech is difficult because only half the lip works.

(Your vigilant editors have thoughtfully edited out my thoughts on this scenario, which, although very brief, are probably unacceptable in even the edgiest publications.)

A week after the operation, the one surgeon who did the exposure told her that what happened was, pure and simple, a surgical mishap. To their credit, they didn't feed us any "oh, it was worse than we thought" surgeon CYA stuff. He told her that in 17 years and hundreds of cases he had never cut the facial nerve removing the roof of the bony canal. He clearly feels awful. Rather than spewing vitriol, she dispensed absolution. She is a better man than I. (That doesn't quite sound right, does it?)

He did tell her that they were able to get the ends of the nerve back together, and that she might have some recovery, with the first signs (if they happen) at 12-18 months. Complete recovery takes seven to 10 years. There is a scale for facial nerve function, with one being normal and six being no movement. She might get to a four, or hopefully a three. Never normal, but maybe below the radar of obvious.

Of course, I found all these people and arranged all these procedures, thinking I would use all my connections and knowledge to make everything right for my baby. Well done, Dad. My brother, who drove from Missoula to Seattle on Thanksgiving Day when he heard what had happened, speculated that he could have gotten the same result after downing a six-pack and using a chain saw. Sensitivity is not big in our family.

I shared my second-guessing with Sally, and in a rather velvety, oxycodone voice she mused, "Is there a more useless emotion than regret?" Uh, well, no.

So now we move ahead. We've always been a fortunate family. Never had a kid in the hospital. I've had a couple scuffs, nothing big, and my parents have lived well into their 80s. We aren't used to bad things, life-changing things, happening to us. Even though I can't yet wrap my mind around this, I know we are going to have to grow.

To experience human existence is to accept mystery. So in hundreds of these cases, why does this one have a technical miscue? Why do seemingly random and very bad things happen to us?

I completely reject the idea that bad things happen to make us tougher or better people. (Another edit.) What I do know is that crisis leads to discovery. The depth of compassion in my friends, colleagues, and you, cherished readers/cheerleaders, has been revelatory. My patients are hilarious. I walk into the room and they say, "I'm fine— you don't need to see my incisions. Tell me everything."

Next time, I will share with you lessons learned from this experience, and how we are approaching this complex rehabilitation.

In the meantime, I have to get back to work. The more patients I see, the more free therapy I get. And sensitivity training isn't cheap.

A Different Christmas

It is Christmas Eve, which for me means I have about four hours of extremely focused holiday preparation, which in turn will hopefully compensate for six weeks of dawdling. There will likely be a lot of gift cards. That certainly demonstrates, on my part, a distinct lack of imagination and emotional effort. However, no one ever returns a gift card.

I have retrieved each of my children, and my wife, on separate midnight flights over the last several days. I hope Santa puts some airline stock under my tree.

I am ever so grateful for each year that we can gather as a family. Many of you face the holidays with the agonizing ache of a loss that can't be reconciled—perhaps the death of a child or a spouse, too soon and oh-so-unfairly taken from you. Perhaps a loved one is lost to drugs or alcohol, or your significant other is just being an idiot.

I sang in the Billings Chorale this last Saturday for the Symphony Christmas concert, and our wonderful soloist Doug Labrecque sang "It's the Most Wonderful Time of the Year." Man, that song can be ironic, can't it?

I have been telling you the story of my daughter Sally—our extensive research regarding her acoustic neuroma, a benign brain tumor; our decision to go ahead finally with a surgical procedure; and the unexpected and frankly disastrous outcome.

I do a fair bit of cancer reconstruction surgery, which I take a special interest in because I know the patients often feel changed or wounded. Supporting them and restoring them is the most important thing I do.

I did not have the brain surgery—Sally did. But if my child is wounded, then I am wounded. As much as I thought I understood physical loss, this is different.

She and I have had extensive discussions about how to respond to this situation. She has, currently, a complete right-side facial paralysis. This is some hope for nerve regeneration there, but her hearing is gone on the right side and won't come back.

After lengthy philosophical discussions, we have boiled the entirety of human experience and suffering into two simple choices. Although we intend to write a book, it will be very short.

Man or mouse. Woman or wimp.

To move forward, you have to make a very hard, cold realization: You've been messed up. You can't change that. Surgery took your leg or breast or your gizzard, chemo took your hair, and pain took the diesel out of your trawler.

So you can be messed up, crawl into an Oxycontin sleeping bag, get your United Victims of America card, and become depressed and isolated.

Or, you can be messed up, turn your sails into the storm that is trying to sink you, and remain engaged and relevant.

You're messed up either way. In one scenario you are lonely and miserable, and in the other you are still suited up and on the floor.

Sally went to her unit Christmas party, has been out every day with people (Mom doesn't count, officially), is off narcotics, and is preparing to go back to work. She still hurts, is frequently nauseated, and is uneasily coming to grips with how people respond to the changes in her speech and appearance. She knows the reality of this injury is going to continue to weigh more heavily with time. In the meantime, she enjoys the fact that her crooked smile totally cracks up a friend's 14-month-old baby. He can't get enough.

I've learned a couple of cool things in addition. Men tend to have rather carefully spaced relationships—that is, we talk about kids and careers, sports and politics, trucks and guns. But when disaster strikes, there is an emergency button that activates a response of caring and love and support that women, who do that on a daily basis, would appreciate.

My guy friends, most of them fathers of daughters, immediately sensed my need, my despair, and did what men do. They got it done. My friend Terry Housinger told me that while women keep the world turning with love and empathy, men emanate power. Sometimes you need a jolt.

This is a community with people of faith. I had literally hundreds of people tell me they were praying for us. I read about how the contemporary intelligencia sees persons of religious or spiritual devotion as sentimental simpletons, that only 13% of Americans attend church, and that believers are declining in numbers precipitously as we become more erudite and educated.

Apparently not here. Billings is a community that scoops up the suffering and supports the sick and prays for the broken. If that is simple and sentimental, then sign me up. (I believe prayer is like radiation—the more focused the better. So, right facial nerve, acoustic canal, middle cranial fossa, Sally Muskett, Seattle, WA.)

For Christmas I wish you hope. Hope for recovery is a large part of our strategy for dealing with difficult realities. Maybe our hopes aren't rational—or realistic.

But how realistic was it for a peasant child, that little light born in a stable in the meanest of circumstances, raised by a carpenter and his wife, to become one of the influential figures in human history?

Christmas is hope, and hope is that light in the darkness of our despair that guides us to acceptance and healing.

In a week I will take them all back. See you at the airport.

Consult Me

"Get this," said Dr. Whitney Robinson while we were hanging out in the surgeon's lounge waiting for our respective cases to start. He was perusing the local paper.

"Blue Cross got sold and they've set up this new foundation. 1.3 million bucks. The guy says, 'It really starts with trying to understand what are the important illnesses within the community...then it's a matter of actually sitting down with the people in the community and deciding what we going to do about this.'"

Even this normally lethargic group of weary surgeons, PAs, and other snacking, snoozing, and texting scrub-suit denizens were roused from their torpor. Comments ensued.

"Give me a cold pack of Miller Lite, and I'll walk through Wal-Mart on Saturday and have the study written up by Monday." That sort of thing.

1.3 million bucks. Hm. My current midlife crisis, Serena, a curvaceous (full figured, I guess you would say, at 56 tons) beauty of seagoing, twin-engined, fiberglass elegance, is listed at 1.2 million. Just right.

I'll bet the owner of Serena would take an offer of 1 million. I would generously save the foundation $300,000.

So I began my study to determine the health care needs of our community, since after at least a thousand such similar studies over the years, we have no idea what our needs might be. I can't tell you how many skinny-suited, hair-gelled, jargon-spouting consultants I've talked to over the years, but it easily exceeds the number of delinquency notices I've received from Medical Records. That's sayin' somethin'.

Obviously I would have to hire my own consultants to establish legitimacy. However, given that Serena's owner is a little dug-in at this point on the price, I can't afford really expensive consultants.

I started with my 20-year-old son, Luke, a sophomore pre-med at the San Diego Country Club—excuse me, University (bikinis around the outdoor pool in February). He said he would do it for $250,000, but after protracted negotiations, including a threat to his Country Club membership, he settled for dinner with two buddies at Red Robin.

"The main threat, as I see it," he opined, Banzai Burger juices forming rivulets on his chin, "to community health is getting old. I recommend against getting old. It seems like everything jumps the tracks with age. You might think trauma gets less frequent as you get less crazy, but then you just trip over your walker."

"The other thing," awaiting another basket of fries, ironically, "is the whole fluffy thing. You get fluffy, and here comes the diabetes, heart disease, joint problems, a lot of cancers, all those leg ulcers you keep whining about as a plastic surgeon, and whatnot."

My next consultant was somewhat less rapacious. Winter Johnson is a fifth-grader at St. Francis Intermediate, and although comfortable with adult conversation, is naïve to the consulting business, and therefore within my budget. I think maybe her dad and mom, Kirk and Katie Hatch, made her do it.

Winter, like Luke, tends to see health issues in broader terms. "Don't do things that will make you stupid." She mentioned drugs (especially the ones that make your teeth fall out), alcohol (car wrecks and getting yourself punched), and texting while you are supposed to be doing something else (driving, for instance). Winter believes in good nutrition ("You are healthy and not fat at the same time.") and hygiene ("Don't sneeze on people, wash your hands, and don't drink icky pool water.")

She also mentioned environmental stewardship: "No Earth, no us." When I asked about cigarettes, she said that King James of England in the 17th century said tobacco made people short of breath. Old James could have gotten quite a grant.

I am heading to Seattle this weekend to check on my Sally. She has gone back to work, and has been fitted with a funky Bluetooth kind of hearing device to help with her missing right ear nerve. Her paralyzed face is continuing to lose tone and slump more, so I just want to lay eyes on her and do a morale assessment.

What has been immeasurably helpful to her is the incredible outpouring of support from you readers. She has read every comment and note you have sent. While she makes no tears on the right side of face, she sure does on the left.

But wait—what a coincidence! The Seattle Boat Show is this weekend! And Serena is there! Given that I have already done the study, and the money is a virtual lock, should I make an offer on the boat? What else does this foundation need to know about health care?

I should probably play it safe. The words of a college dude and a fifth-grader will probably fly right over their heads.

Childhood Trauma

I think my traumatic childhood began when I was about 31 years old. Up until then, things had been pretty conventional: loving parents, every advantage—the white, male, middle-class, American Dream.

Then came my cardiac surgery training at Washington University. My faculty professors were tantrum-throwing, instrument-hurling, and profanely screaming, emotional basket cases. I should have enough PTSD to fill three *American Sniper* movies.

When I came to work in Billings, I couldn't figure out what was wrong. My senior partners were calm and efficient, and never yelled or screamed. Once, on a particularly difficult reoperation, we cut a hole in the heart, which lead to some pretty noisy bleeding. Tim just calmly put a finger in the hole, and then asked if someone would mind terribly putting that new CD in the music player.

It was a revelation to me that you could actually do heart surgery with about as much stress and fuss as putting your socks into the laundry.

Pretty much all of our emotional responses to the events in our lives are learned. Look at the toddler who falls down and bumps his head. If Mom or Dad freaks out, the kid freaks out. If we are cool, the kid blows it off. That holds true for 31 year-olds, too.

I learned that my emotions and attitudes were pretty much what I made them.

I had a great weekend in Seattle with my daughter. My big grant studying health care needs hasn't come through, so I didn't buy anything at the boat show. But I had a normal and wonderful weekend hanging out with my daughter. What was normal about it was that she and I did everything we usually would do: eating out, walking around, and boring boat brokers who know I will never actually fork over the cash.

She has decided to do everything she normally does—go to parties, go to work, go to boat shows, meet and greet—that she did before the surgery that left her with her face paralyzed and her right-sided hearing gone.

And it was fine.

I set very few restrictions on my patients. What I have found is that if they actually do something normal, they don't feel sick or wounded. "I went to my kid's basketball game the day after surgery!" "I walked three miles this weekend after I just got out of the hospital!" Their actions are telling them that they aren't damaged.

Although it is important to get feedback from others in our lives, the most important feedback we get is from ourselves. In times of illness or disability, the biggest factor in our sense of well-being is not how we feel, but what we do.

It is easy to sit in bed and say, "I don't feel well. I am sick." Sitting in bed reinforces that. Or you stay home from an event or a game or a night out because you hurt or "don't feel well." So, you aren't well.

I deal with many courageous patients who have terrible arthritis, awful internal diseases, and even terminal illnesses, and they resemble the Energizer Bunny on crack. "Well," one remarkable lady told me, "I can hurt in the game or hurt on the bench. May as well be a player."

You can always talk yourself into avoiding things. You can avoid your whole life if you want. A lot of people do that with pills or blow or alcohol. What is most impactful in getting ourselves through difficult times in not Self Talking—it is Self Doing.

If you are low after a surgery or an illness, take a walk. Go to a movie. Show up somewhere. Be a player. Go up to some boat salesman with half your face paralyzed and ask him why the owner took one trip on a brand new boat and then put it up for sale. Show yourself that an injury or illness won't define who or what you are.

Don't talk to yourself. Show yourself. Just as others view us—it isn't what we say we are—we are (getting all existential here) what we do.

I don't think I am going to get much sympathy or compensation for my PTSD. No one is going to make a movie about my suffering.

I guess I'll just take a walk.

Crazy

"I think I might be going crazy."

I am used to phone calls in the middle of the night—someone has a fever, needs a different pain medication, or perhaps some extra IV fluid.

Not calls from my children.

We've been concerned about our daughter Sally, of course, as the psychological toll of the facial paralysis she suffered after brain-tumor surgery is known to be devastating. Going crazy wouldn't be much of a stretch.

"The last few days people at work tell me I look a lot better. Then one of the other nurses said she saw my face move. I don't know."

I got out of bed and fired up Face Time on my computer. I was able to see on the screen a faint but clearly discernable uh, well, yes... a smile.

In addition, the pronounced sag on the paralyzed side was gone, and the droopy lower eyelid was tightening up. I made her do every facial nerve gyration I know about 50 times. No question.

She is five months postop, and all the experts I have pestered relentlessly told me there would be nothing before nine months. We got a picture today, on Facebook of course, of her at the "Run for the Babies" in Seattle, which she helped organize. She is holding some plump little former preemie, and very clearly smiling—a little smile, a crooked smile, the two eyes not the same shape, but, you know, you wouldn't call it anything else but a smile.

My breast reconstruction patients often tell me what a big difference there is between something, even if it isn't the greatest, and nothing. I really understand that now.

Of course now we are greedy, getting hooked up with neuroscientists and therapists who specialize in brain and nerve retraining, so that as the nerve repairs, things move the way they are supposed to. A big problem in this situation is that that the wire to the garbage disposal gets hooked up to the microwave. The brain has to get used to the reality that all those nerves/wires are not where they used to be.

We know intellectually that there is no chance she will ever be entirely normal. Emotionally, we're going after every neuron that isn't nailed down.

We notified the two surgeons involved of the change. No response—they've moved on. Note to young providers: When you have a problem with a procedure or therapy, bring that patient closer—don't distance yourself. The patients I've been closest to are the ones where we have had to fight through a problem together. The last thing a suffering person needs is abandonment.

I can no longer count the number of people who have told me they are praying for her recovery. I don't believe in a god that gives people tumors to somehow challenge them personally, or that God changes the scoreboard. But there is also no question in my mind that so much concentrated faith and love and attention is healing. For those of you out there who have been on Sally's case—be proud. You've done something very special, and very real. Keep it up.

Dr. Margaret Beeson at the Yellowstone Naturopathic Clinic assigned her residents in training the task of studying nerve recovery, and Sally has been assiduously following a program of supplements and physiotherapy. To have a plan and a direction is a blessing when you feel otherwise helpless and wounded.

Healing is about using all your resources and bringing all your assets to the process of becoming well. Not just fixed, but well. Physical fitness, nutrition, spirituality, attitude, character, family—and, unfortunately, luck—all enter in the equation. All that, and hoping your surgeon is having a good day.

To heal others? Sometimes it is just about keeping that person close. Close in your thoughts, in your prayers, in your research, in your cheerleading, or in your quiet presence.

The thing about crazy? It can be pretty cool.

Made in the USA
Lexington, KY
03 April 2017